The Complexities of American Indian Identity in the Twenty-First Century

The Complexities of American Indian Identity in the Twenty-First Century

Sean M. Daley and Christine Makosky Daley
With Ryan Goeckner and Jason Hale

LEXINGTON BOOKS
Lanham • Boulder • New York • London

Published by Lexington Books
An imprint of The Rowman & Littlefield Publishing Group, Inc.
4501 Forbes Boulevard, Suite 200, Lanham, Maryland 20706
www.rowman.com

86-90 Paul Street, London EC2A 4NE

British Library Cataloguing in Publication Information Available

Library of Congress Cataloging-in-Publication Data

Names: Daley, Sean M., 1973- author. | Makosky Daley, Christine, 1974-
author.
Title: The complexities of American Indian identity in the twenty-first
century / Sean M. Daley and Christine Makosky Daley.
Other titles: Complexities of American Indian identity in the 21st century
Description: Lanham : Lexington Books, [2023] | Includes bibliographical
references and index. | Summary: "Drawing on data and stories from
Native 24/7, a 5-year, 700-particpant social investigation of Indigenous
identity, the authors document what Native people believe characterizes,
constitutes, and contributes to contemporary Native identities"—
Provided by publisher.
Identifiers: LCCN 2022055528 (print) | LCCN 2022055529 (ebook) | ISBN
9781793643872 (cloth ; alk. paper) | ISBN 9781793643889 (electronic)
Subjects: LCSH: Indians of North America—Ethnic identity—History—21st
century. | Indians of North America—Social life and customs—21st
century. | Indians of North America—Tribal citizenship.
Classification: LCC E98.E85 D35 2023 (print) | LCC E98.E85 (ebook) | DDC
305.897—dc23/eng/20221123
LC record available at https://lccn.loc.gov/2022055528
LC ebook record available at https://lccn.loc.gov/2022055529

♾️™ The paper used in this publication meets the minimum requirements of
American National Standard for Information Sciences—Permanence of Paper
for Printed Library Materials, ANSI/NISO Z39.48-1992.

~

Contents

~

Figures

~

Tables

~

Preface

Our team has been working together conducting research with and providing service to Native communities throughout the United States for over fifteen years. Some members of our team have been doing so for ten years longer than that and other members of our team are Native and have been members of their respective communities for their entire lives; in several cases over forty years. Over time, we have received countless comments from other academics about the need to quantify "American Indian identity or ties to culture." We have also been asked how we "know" that the people who participate in our research are "actually Native" when we use self-report status of race/ethnicity rather than asking for a Tribal Enrollment Card or Certificate of Degree of Indian Blood. Reviewers for multiple funding agencies have requested that we add measures of acculturation to our studies, and reviewers of our academic manuscripts have questioned how we can call programs we develop culturally appropriate if we do not measure culture in some way. Academics who listen to our presentations at national conferences do the same. We are confident that we are not alone in our receipt of these comments. We are also confident that people who work with other cultural, racial, or ethnic groups in the United States do not get asked these questions.

Members of our team who have participated in grant reviews have never heard a reviewer question how someone knows that the people in their study are of African American or Latin American heritage. There may be a question about measuring acculturation of immigrants and there are validated scales for precisely that. But there is no question about how to determine that a person is Mexican American or African American or Japanese American; that is taken as fact once the person says it. Why the difference? Why do we need proof that our participants are who they say they are? Does it simply come down to the fact that Native people do not all "look" the stereotypic way others think they should? Or is it about the fact that we CAN ask for a card and others cannot?

The real answer to all of this is that we know our participants are Native because the people on our team and the people with whom we work tell us they are Native, not because we can quantify it or because we determined that some artificial stereotype of "what an Indian should look like" is correct. We do not ask for Tribal Enrollment Cards or Certificates of Degree of Indian Blood because we know that not all Native people have the ability to get them nor do they all want them. We know that no piece of paper truly determines who is Native, though it can be a source of pride and a way to access needed services. We also know that there is no skin tone, facial shape, eye shape, hair color or texture, or any other physical feature that defines a Native person. Native people, like every other cultural, racial, or ethnic group are hugely heterogeneous in their looks, beliefs and worldviews, and ways of life, as it should be in any thriving cultural group. It is precisely the heterogeneity of all of these things that makes contemporary Native people who they are.

We do not and will not measure "Indianness" as if it is the same as acculturation of immigrants. Moving to another country, whether it is of your own free will or for other factors, is inherently different from being in a colonial situation. Measuring how much Native people are like the dominant culture is akin to measuring the success of colonization and Termination. We have made a collective decision not to do that. If we find a measure of ties to a particular Native community or culture that we and our community colleagues want to use or if we create one ourselves, we may use it. However, it will not be a measure of acculturation, and we will never use it to determine whether or not someone is Native and allowed to participate in our studies. If this hurts us with reviewers for funding agencies or journals or with our peer academics overall, so be it.

In response to the many comments we have received about the need to prove who has a rightful place in our work, we decided to ask people from different communities how they wanted to be defined. Initially, we planned to talk with our community advisors for our research about what to do and simply listen to them and move on. We also had several Native college and graduate students with whom we planned to talk and whom we wanted to involve in the process. After initial discussions with these groups, we realized that there was a need for research in this area and that Native people around us had voices that they wanted to be heard on the topic. A plan for a few simple discussions to answer reviewer concerns led to a four-year study during which we talked with over seven hundred Native people from all over the country about contemporary Native identity. The pages that follow describe the results of this study, focused on the vibrancy and heterogeneity of "Indianness" in today's world. The answer to "Who is an Indian?" is that there is no one "Native American" culture and no one "right way" to be an American Indian. Tribal Enrollment Cards and Certificates of Degree of Indian Blood do not determine who is an Indian. Physical characteristics do not determine who is Native. Indigenous people are as varied as all people, and their contemporary identities should be recognized as such.

Participant views of these simple questions about cultural connectedness provide a glimpse into the pages that follow, which focus primarily on what *Native 24/7* participants said in their interviews. We focus on the words of participants to present their views as clearly as possible. In chapter 2, participants tell us about the terms that they would prefer others use to describe their racial or ethnic category. Chapter 3 delves into participants' thoughts on culture, history, and heritage, and the roles they play in contemporary Native identity. Chapter 4 explores the connections among family, community, and relationships and identity. Chapter 5 investigates religion and spirituality and their connections to modern Native identity. Chapter 6 looks at participants' views of Certificate of Degree of Indian Blood Cards and tribal enrollment. Finally, chapter 7 attempts to provide some type of conclusion about what it means to be American Indian/Native American/ Indian/Native/Indigenous/insert tribal name/etc. in contemporary America.

~

Acknowledgments

The authors would like to thank and acknowledge the following individuals for their assistance with the *Native 24/7* project, including administering surveys, assisting with interviews, transcribing and coding interviews, data entry, literature reviews, and numerous other tasks not mentioned here:

- Justin Begaye (Navajo)
- Kelly Berryhill (Sac and Fox)
- Shelley Bointy (Dakota/Ottawa/Assiniboine)
- Stacy Braiuca (Citizen Band Potawatomi)
- Isaiah Brokenleg (Sicangu Lakota)
- Travis Brown (Sac and Fox/Kiowa)
- Anna Carson
- Angel Cully (Chippewa/Ioway)
- Lance Cully (Seminole/Ft. Sill Apache)
- Maggie Davis
- Sharon Eagleman (Dakota/Ottawa/Assiniboine)
- Melissa Filippi
- Matthew Frank (Navajo)
- Jordyn Gunville (Cheyenne River Sioux)
- River Gunville (Cheyenne River Sioux)
- Aysia Gusman (Quapaw)
- Caitlin Haas
- Christina Haswood (Navajo)

- Sumanth Jain-Wasburn
- JB Kinlacheeny (Navajo)
- Rachel Lackey (Cherokee)
- Charlotte McCloskey (Sicangu Lakota)
- Tiyana Murphy (Navajo)
- Christina Pacheco (Cherokee of Oklahoma/Quechua of Bolivia)
- Ronnie Raney
- Dasy Resendiz
- Matthew Roach
- Julia Soap (Cherokee of Oklahoma/Prairie Band of Potawatomi)
- Cheree Solomon (Navajo)
- Nya Smith (Navajo/Osage)
- T. Edward Smith (Osage)
- Rina Stabler (Ioway/Omaha)
- Myrietta Talawyma (Hopi/Ioway)
- Stephen Valliere (Lac Du Flambeau Chippewa)
- Julian Wahnee (Comanche/Navajo)
- Julia White Bull (Cheyenne River Sioux/Oglala Lakota)
- Chandler Williams (Muskogee Creek)
- Crisandra Wilkie (Turtle Mountain Chippewa)
- And any other individuals whom we may have inadvertently forgotten

The authors would also like to thank and acknowledge the following individuals and committees for their financial support:

- Dr. Won S. Choi, Department of Population Health, University of Kansas Medical Center, Kansas City, Kansas
- Jim Lane, Dean of the Division of Arts, Design, Humanities, and Social Sciences, Johnson County Community College, Overland Park, Kansas
- The 2015 Faculty Sabbatical Committee, Johnson County Community College, Overland Park, Kansas

The authors would like to thank the numerous powwow and event committees throughout the United States who allowed us to administer surveys and conduct interviews at their gatherings. A'ho.

~

CHAPTER ONE

Methods and Participants

Who is an Indian? This was the question that began the development of the research presented through this text. There is no simple answer, and the things that influence how a person identifies himself or herself are numerous. The reader who wants to jump into the answers to the question should jump straight to chapter 2; those who wish to understand the methods behind the study, how it was developed, and who the participants were should read on. Either way, the participants of *Native 24/7* teach the true heterogeneity of contemporary Native peoples of the United States.

Methods

In 2010, our research team decided to undertake a research study to understand contemporary Native identity. The original plan was to talk with our Community Advisory Board and do some additional interviews to get a picture of identity in our region (Southern Plains bridging into the Midwest and Northern Plains). We started to talk with a few Native students who were working with the team about how we should approach this task, hoping that they would take some ownership of the process and the project itself. The students were not from our region and immediately wanted to broaden the scope to include other regions of the country because they believed there were differences by region. We continued discussions, including more of our research team, recognizing that the students would not be able to conduct the study in its entirety if it was going to be a lot bigger. Over the course of about three months, our simple study that was going to be a few interviews and a discussion with our Community Advisory Board members turned into something much bigger. We did not have a primary funding source specifically for this research project; however, we had some funds attached to our research center that could be used for advertisement of our programs through things like T-shirts and other small incentives. We decided to use those funds to provide hooded sweatshirts to eligible participants as a thank you for participation.

Once we had established the basic idea that we would collect demographic information with a survey and then conduct interviews, we came up with a list of questions and a beginning sampling frame, which we presented to our Community Advisory Board, made up of ten individuals representing the local community. Our initial meeting did not go as planned. The local Native community was very heterogeneous, with over two hundred different tribes represented and people from urban, suburban, and reservation communities represented, as well as people who were enrolled and people who were not. This diverse community was precisely the reason we had always asked people to self-identify as Native for all of our projects. Our two-hour meeting, which had several other things planned for the agenda, was quickly taken over by this first topic. We spent nearly three hours together, talking through the types of things about which we needed to ask and how to develop a sampling frame, sometimes contentiously. Comments were made such as, "Well, if you don't talk to only people on the reservation, you're going to get false positives," meaning that those individuals who claimed to be Native and did not grow up on a reservation should not be considered American Indians. Some board members believed only "card-carrying Indians" should be included, referring to Tribal Enrollment Cards. Others felt only elders should be included because they know "what it truly means to be Native American." Others opposed these ideas, wanting more of a focus on urban communities who they felt were ignored.

That meeting brought us back to the drawing board, and we began a more systematic and rigorous study design process using community-based participatory research. In this research framework, community members are included throughout the process (Israel et al. 1998). All of our research has always used it, and this study, in many ways, was our most inclusive and most collaborative, even though it was also the most contentious. The contentiousness became a motivating factor for doing it to the best of our abilities and having long discussions among researchers (many, though not all, of whom were Native themselves), students, and advisors, including both community and academic. We spent the better part of a year holding discussions and writing and rewriting survey and interview questions and establishing a sampling frame, albeit a flawed one, but the best one we could create. We included many factors and tried to get a representative sample to understand this complex topic. Our final conclusions for design of the study are included below.

Sampling Frame

The first and most obvious decision to us was to include anyone who self-identified as Native American, American Indian, or any other term that could describe people whose pre-Columbian ancestry in some way came from what is now the United States. Participants did not have to be "100%" Native or enrolled in a federally recognized or state-recognized tribe. As noted by Jacobs and Merolla (2017), "The standards used to judge whether Indian identities are acceptable (or authentic) are based on romanticized versions of Indianness that are static, essentialist, and reductive. These nearly unattainable constructions of Indianness are perpetuated within political and cultural spheres because they serve the dominant group's interests" (65). We followed this idea and used self-identification as our inclusion criterion.

We decided to stratify by four factors, including gender (male, female, and other), age (18–29, 30–49, and 50+), location where individuals grew up (reservation, rural non-reservation, and urban non-reservation), and culture area. The United States was divided using a culture area approach (Wissler 1927). This stratification system created a large sampling frame, which we modified over time. Our first modification took place before our first interview. We decided to include only male and female in gender for the purposes of creating the sampling frame, though we included a third category with a write-in option on the demographic survey. We chose not to actively pursue recruitment of individuals who did not identify as either male or female for the purposes of filling a stratum, but rather would include all people and determine post hoc how analysis of additional genders would be handled. In essence, individuals who identified outside of male or female would be placed outside of our sampling frame and potentially analyzed separately. Our reasoning for this decision was twofold: (1) We were concerned about an already extremely large sampling frame and needed to decrease it and were concerned about recruitment efforts in this area; and (2) this study was not meant to be focused on non-binary gendered individuals, and we were concerned that we would not be able to do justice to that community. We firmly believe that a study focused entirely on this population is needed and should be done.

We stratified next by age, which we divided into three categories for the purpose of developing the sampling frame: 18–29, 30–49, and 50+. Though this also an imperfect division, we chose it because we were attempting to represent certain stages of life and viewpoints. We first decided not to include children under age eighteen and to focus instead on adult perspectives, recognizing the challenges of including children in any research and our own need to keep the scope of the project somewhat narrow. We believe this is another study that is very needed. The first of the three strata in the age category was selected to represent young adults, with the intent of capturing college students and non-college students, though not specifically stratified for that. The second was intended to capture parents and working adults, as well as the generation of people raised by those who had attended boarding schools. The final age category was intended to capture people who had already raised children, might have grandchildren, and might have attended boarding schools. We considered splitting this category to ensure that we captured enough elders of an older generation (possible age 70+) but decided not to, given the younger age distribution of Native people nationwide and because of concerns regarding the size of our potential sample.

We decided to stratify our sample by where an individual grew up rather than where they were currently living. This was done after significant deliberation with the ultimate decision being made based on the idea that an individual's formative years are extremely important to identity development. We stratified in this area by two factors: the area of the country in which the person was raised and whether or not someone grew up in a tribal community, either a reservation or tribal trust land. Reservations and tribal trust land communities were combined into a single stratum because it would be impossible to have both represented in all geographic areas. Though these types of communities are not entirely the same and growing up on them cannot be seen as identical, we decided that they were more similar to each other than to other areas because they are primarily Native communities. There was much discussion over this point and the decision to bring them together was not unanimous, thus on our demographic survey we separated them, even though they were lumped together for stratification purposes. Individuals off the reservation were stratified by whether they lived in a rural or urban environment. Suburban communities were lumped together with urban for ease and to keep the sample size from getting out of hand.

The final stratification was done based on area of the country in which the person grew up. We divided the country into culture areas based on the original work of Clark Wissler who divided the United States into areas based on regional differences in material culture and social behavior (Wissler 1927).

We made some modifications to the original map and included the following areas: Arctic, California, Great Basin, Great Lakes, Northeast, Northwest Coast, Northern Plains, Plateau, Southeast, Southern Plains, Southwest, and Subarctic. We elected not to include Native Hawaiian peoples because their cultures are distinctly different and more similar to other Pacific Island communities than Native peoples on the mainland. These areas are somewhat different from what is normally seen. For example, the Plains are sometimes grouped together; we preferred to separate them into Northern and Southern based on differences in the tribal nations in these regions, particularly in present day. The Southern Plains, Oklahoma in particular, is an area with a huge diversity of tribal nations, including many groups who were moved there during forced relocation. The area is known for a blending of different Native cultures into a distinctly different culture area than the Northern Plains. We chose to break the Great Lakes area apart from the Northeast and the Northeast apart from the Southeast; some versions of the culture areas of North America combine some or all of these regions. Figure 1.1 shows how we defined the culture areas for the purposes of *Native 24/7*.

Native 24/7 Project Culture Area Map

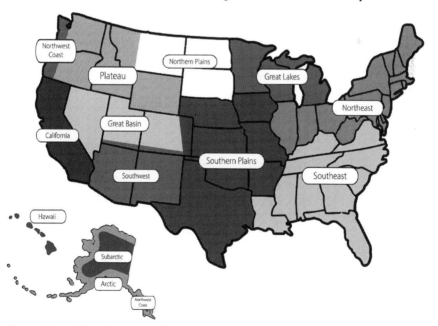

Figure 1.1. Culture Areas. *Credit*: Sean M. Daley, Luke Swimmer, and Julia White Bull.

The areas seen in figure 1.1 were our original planned culture areas for stratification. After beginning recruitment and identifying difficulties in recruitment based on our ability to identify participants and travel to only certain parts of the country, we collapsed some culture areas as follows: (1) Northeast and Southeast were combined; (2) Northwest Coast, Arctic, and Subarctic were grouped together; and (3) Great Basin and Plateau were grouped together. Figure 1.2 represents one culture area of our sampling frame; this sampling frame was duplicated in each of the listed culture areas. We planned for three interviews per stratum, for a total of 54 participants in each of 8 culture areas, or a grand total of 432 participants.

Development of Survey and Interview Questions

We decided to conduct interviews with an accompanying survey of demographic characteristics and a few questions about beliefs about following Native ways of life. Full questions and answer choices can be found in table 1.1. The survey was developed over a year and included numerous revisions and several complete redraftings. Our team and community advisors went back and forth over whether or not to include different demographic information and if we should include any questions on beliefs or include any scales used to measure acculturation, identity, ties to culture, etc. We examined many of these scales and each was met with criticism from our community partners. What we ultimately created was a short survey collecting far less information than we initially planned. We decided it was more important to get people

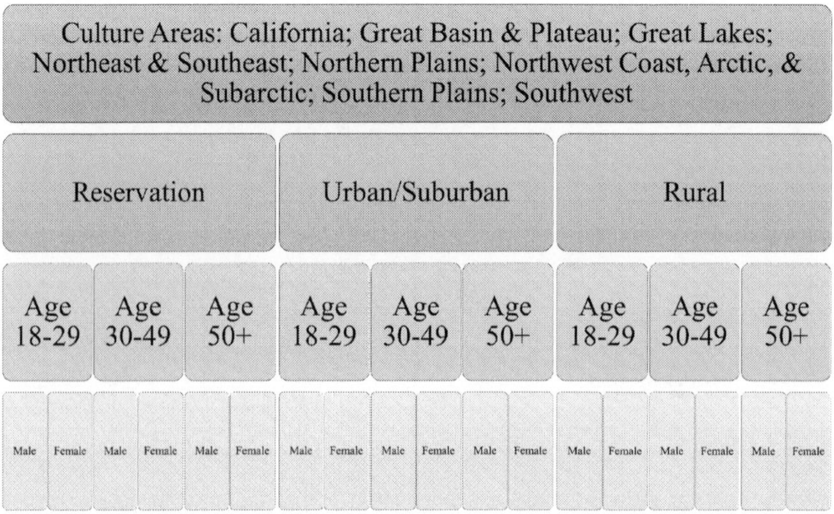

Culture Areas: California; Great Basin & Plateau; Great Lakes; Northeast & Southeast; Northern Plains; Northwest Coast, Arctic, & Subarctic; Southern Plains; Southwest								
Reservation			Urban/Suburban			Rural		
Age 18-29	Age 30-49	Age 50+	Age 18-29	Age 30-49	Age 50+	Age 18-29	Age 30-49	Age 50+
Male Female	Male Female	Male Female	Male Female	Male Female	Male Female	Male Female	Male Female	Male Female

Figure 1.2. Sampling Frame for One Culture Area. *Credit*: Christine M. Daley.

into our interviews; that was where we planned to collect the majority of information. We wanted a very short survey that would not be burdensome or dissuade people from participating in the interview. We also wanted one that would pique people's interest in the topic, hopefully drawing them into the interview.

We asked about gender, age, race/ethnicity, tribal affiliation(s), enrollment status, current relationship status, race/ethnicity of parents and spouse or significant other/partner, number of children (if any), employment status (yes or no only), and educational attainment. We chose specifically not to include income level because many of our advisors told us that would be a sensitive topic for many people and we did not have a clear reason to include it. We also asked people where they grew up for the purpose of putting them into our sampling frame.

To begin to understand beliefs about following various Native ways of life, we asked a series of questions about participation in traditional activities, living in traditional ways, and maintenance of Native identity and values. We also asked about speaking a Native language, and friendships with other Native people. We did not intend these questions to provide a full picture of identity, but rather to give us some understanding and allow us to make comparisons of these items with information that came out in the interviews.

Table 1.1. Survey Questions

Question	Answer Choices
What is your gender?	Male Female Fill-in
What is your age?	Fill-in
Which one more of the following describes your ethnicity or race? Check all that apply.	American Indian/Alaska Native Black/African American Asian Latino/Hispanic Native Hawaiian/Other Pacific Islander White Fill-in
What is (are) your tribal affiliation?	Fill-in
Are you an enrolled member of your tribe?	Yes No
Race/ethnicity of your mother. Check all that apply.	American Indian/Alaska Native Black/African American Asian Latino/Hispanic Native Hawaiian/Other Pacific Islander White Fill-in

(continued)

Table 1.1. *(continued)*

Question	Answer Choices
Race/ethnicity of your father. Check all that apply.	American Indian/Alaska Native Black/African American Asian Latino/Hispanic Native Hawaiian/Other Pacific Islander White Fill-in
Race/ethnicity of your spouse or significant other/partner. Check all that apply.	American Indian/Alaska Native Black/African American Asian Latino/Hispanic Native Hawaiian/Other Pacific Islander White Fill-in
Some families have special activities or traditions that take place every year at particular times, such as holiday gatherings, special meals or giveaways, religious activities, healing ceremonies, or honoring powwows. How many of these special activities or traditions does your family take part in based on . . .	
Your Native culture	Not at all A few Some A lot
Other Native cultures	Not at all A few Some A lot
Non-Native cultures	Not at all A few Some A lot
Some people talk about living life in traditional ways. To what extent do you follow . . .	
The Native way of life	Not at all Rarely Sometimes A lot
The non-Native way of life	Not at all Rarely Sometimes A lot

Question	Answer Choices
How well do you speak the language of your tribe or Nation?	I don't speak my language
	I speak it a little, but not very well
	I speak it moderately
	I speak my Native language very well
How many of your close friends are . . .	
From your Nation	None
	Some of them
	Most of them
	All or nearly all
From other Nations	None
	Some of them
	Most of them
	All or nearly all
Non-Native	None
	Some of them
	Most of them
	All or nearly all
How important is it to you that you maintain . . .	
Your Native identity, and your Nations' values and practices	Not at all
	A little
	Somewhat
	Very much
Other Natives' values and practices	Not at all
	A little
	Somewhat
	Very much
Non-Natives values and practices	Not at all
	A little
	Somewhat
	Very much
How important is it to you that members of your immediate family maintain . . .	
Your Native identity, and your Nations' values and practices	Not at all
	A little
	Somewhat
	Very much
Other Natives' values and practices	Not at all
	A little
	Somewhat
	Very much
Non-Natives values and practices	Not at all
	A little
	Somewhat
	Very much

(continued)

Table 1.1. *(continued)*

Question	Answer Choices
Where did you grow up? Choose all that apply.	On a reservation On tribal trust land In a rural area (off reservation) In an urban area (off reservation) In a suburban area (off reservation) Fill-in
If more than two were identified, which one was your primary?	Fill-in
Where did you grow up specifically?	Fill-in
What is your current relationship status?	Married or in a relationship Divorced, separated, or widowed Never married Fill-in
Do you have children? How many?	Yes, fill-in number No
Are you currently employed?	Yes No
What is the highest grade or year of school you completed?	Elementary/Grade School Some high school High school graduate/GED Post-high school certification Some College 2-year college graduate (AA/AS degree) 4-year college graduate (BA/BS degree) Graduate degree (please list) Never attended school

Credit: Christine M. Daley

Interview questions were created using the same process of meeting with research team members and Community Advisory Board members for about a year. The original list of questions for interviews had nearly fifty questions and probably would have taken hours to discuss with each participant. After many iterations of the questions, we determined that we wanted only a few grand tour or large, open-ended questions. These would be asked of every participant, and follow-up questions would be determined by the interviewer during the interview. We hoped that using this semistructured technique would encourage participants to talk about the things that were important to them rather than focus only on things important to the interviewer. We ended up with a total of eight open-ended questions, as follows:

1. Do you prefer a particular term to describe your ethnicity (i.e., Native American, American Indian, Alaska Native, Indian, Name of Tribe/ Nation, etc.)?
2. What does being (preferred term from #1) mean to you?
3. What do you feel truly sets (preferred term from #1) people apart from others in the United States?
4. Does religion or spirituality affect your view of your identity?
5. Who or what has influenced you the most with your identity (i.e., particular person, events, governments, society, family, history, stories, etc.)? How has that person/thing/event influenced your identity?
6. What are your feelings about Certificate of Degree of Indian Blood (CDIB) cards?
7. Is there anything you would like to add?
8. Is there anything that I did not ask that you wish I had?

We ended the interview by asking participants if they could recommend anyone else who might want to participate. Interviewees were invited to provide contact information for someone else if they would like or to provide our contact information to friends and family.

Recruitment and Data Collection

Methods of recruitment were determined primarily by our Native team members and Community Advisory Board members. One of our Native team members created a logo for the project, which we put on hooded sweatshirts to give to participants. Because this was a primarily unfunded project, we did not provide additional incentives. We decided that interviews would be conducted by our Native team members because we were concerned that community members may not be willing to talk about certain aspects of their identity with non-Native people. We began with a convenience sample of people we knew in the local and regional community, followed by people we knew outside of our region. Initial interviews were conducted in-person with paper demographic surveys filled out prior to the interview. As we moved outside of our region, we decided to also allow telephone interviews. For these, we asked people to fill out the survey online prior to the interview. We used SurveyMonkey® for survey data collection. Telephone interviews were recorded using the Ring Central® secure telephone system with cloud storage. At the end of each interview, we asked the participant to identify others who might be interested in participating, thus allowing snowball sampling.

We began a second method of recruitment shortly after starting the project, using community events that we attended, including powwows and other social events, health fairs, and back-to-school fairs across the country. We had tables at the events with electronic data collection devices with internet access for completing surveys (e.g., laptops, tablet computers, etc.) and conducted live, recorded interviews at the events using noise-cancelling microphones. When Wi-Fi internet service was not available, we used either a mobile hotspot or paper surveys. Where appropriate, we used announcements by event emcees to draw potential participants to our table. These interviews were primarily conducted by Native team members, with some of our non-Native team members assisting with the surveys and general recruitment at the events. In a few cases, when tables got extremely busy, we used non-Native team members to conduct interviews with participants who stated that they were willing to talk with someone who was not Native. Hosting tables at events was our most successful recruitment method.

To reach additional people around the country, we turned to student interns. In each year of the study, we had between ten and twenty-five student interns for a summer internship that we regularly held. The majority of our interns were Native from different regions of the United States. During the internship, students worked on multiple research projects with our team, including *Native 24/7*. For this project, they recruited friends and family in the same way that our team did at the beginning of the project. Additional snowball sampling expanded the sample. Because we had interns from around the country, we were able to recruit from places that were further away and for which we could not get to in-person events. This broadened our sample dramatically.

We learned quickly throughout recruitment that it was going to be difficult to keep track of the exact number of people participating in a given stratum in an immediate way, particularly when we were recruiting at large events and when we had multiple interns recruiting at the same time. We also learned that three individuals per stratum was not nearly enough to saturate the data (i.e., to come to a point where we were not getting any additional major themes through added recruitment) (Bernard 2017). In fact, we could not always measure saturation in a timely fashion to tell us when to stop recruitment of a particular stratum. We made the decision to assess our sample and potential saturation of the data every few months or after large recruitment events. As we assessed, we closed individual strata to recruitment. There were times, however, where we had willing participants at events from closed strata whom we did not want to turn away and continued to allow to participate. We did this primarily because we did not want to stop someone from talking about his or her identity if he or she was willing. We did not like the idea of turning people away when they had something to say. Therefore, our sample became more heavily weighted to certain culture areas where we were able to attend larger events. This influenced our findings and we tried to account for it through analysis by different demographic variables, including culture area.

Interviews with accompanying surveys were conducted between May 23, 2011, and January 30, 2015, and lasted on average between ten and twenty minutes with a range of five to sixty minutes. We had a total of 734 participants in the survey and 636 participants in the interviews. The reason we had more participants in the survey was because at some larger events, we did not get to all of the interviews. Participants were invited to complete their interview via a telephone call and in some cases did, but not all completed it. Some participants filled out the survey, left to do something else at the event while waiting for us to be ready for them (e.g., dance during a powwow), and then decided not the return to complete the interview. There were also some instances (98 participants) when a participant was interviewed before completing the survey and somehow did not complete the survey, likely due to difficulties in managing recruitment at the larger events.

A total of twenty-five individual interviewers were used throughout the project. Some were better able than others to draw out information from participants, leading to better data in some cases. Though, in an ideal world, the same person would have conducted all of the interviews, it was not possible in a study this size. Given limited funding and a need to end the study, we stopped recruitment before completing our sampling frame. Our total number of participants was higher than planned but did not fill every stratum. Even with our limitations in data collection, we believe that there is much to learn from participants about the heterogeneity of contemporary identity. We believe that further research will only enhance what we have begun.

Data Analysis

Because we collected both survey and interview data, we planned quantitative and qualitative analyses. Initially, we planned quantitative analyses for survey data and qualitative for interview data. However, we decided that we wanted to be able to look across survey and interview data for the same individual. Therefore, we also included a quantitative analysis of our interview data, leaving us with a mixed methods analysis. All survey data were collected via either SurveyMonkey® or on paper. Interns with our team entered data collected via paper forms into SurveyMonkey®. Each survey was first entered by one intern and then checked by a second to ensure accuracy. All data were then compiled into one spreadsheet for analysis. The quantitative analysis for this project was generated using SAS software, Version 9.4 Copyright © 2016. All interviews were recorded using either our secure telephone system or digital voice recorders. Interns with our team transcribed all the interviews verbatim for analysis. Transcripts were checked against the recordings by research team members, who also corrected them as needed.

To ensure the ability to conduct both a qualitative text analysis and a quantitative content analysis of the interview data, we coded the data twice. For text analysis, we used a modified version of a community-based participatory research technique that we developed over the course of three previous focus group studies with a total of seventy-two focus groups and 519 individual participants (Makosky Daley et al. 2010). For this technique, we needed five individuals involved in the analysis of each culture area, including three coders and two thematic reviewers. We could not use the same coders and reviewers for all culture areas because of the rules we place on coders and reviewers. We include primary, secondary, and tertiary coders, all formally trained in qualitative methods, but with different perspectives and different roles (see figure 1.3). Because our secondary coders provide an emic or insider's perspective, these individuals should fit into the stratum being analyzed. We did not have people on our team who fit into each stratum. Therefore, we had to select what characteristic(s) were most important to providing an emic understanding. We decided that being Native and having been raised in a Native culture (on a reservation or not on a reservation) were the most important factors, followed by the area of the country in which a person grew up, using our culture area approach. We believed that culture area would be important particularly for understanding colloquial language when conducting analysis. We divided the transcripts based on culture area and selected our coders for each culture area. The primary and tertiary coders did not have to follow the rules for an emic perspective. In all cases, we used Native people who had been raised in a Native culture as secondary or emic coders, but we were unable to always match culture area based on who was on our team. When we could not match culture area, we chose to use someone who had either spent some time in the culture area or grew up in an adjacent culture area. There was overlap among individuals coding different culture areas and we wound up with a total of fifteen coders.

All coders met to develop a codebook which was then used throughout all analysis. They coded the transcripts inductively and came up with initial ideas of themes in the data, which were then compiled into a set of thematic statements by the primary coder (etic perspective), with assistance from the secondary coder (emic perspective). All coders for each culture area identified potential representative quotes from participants; the secondary

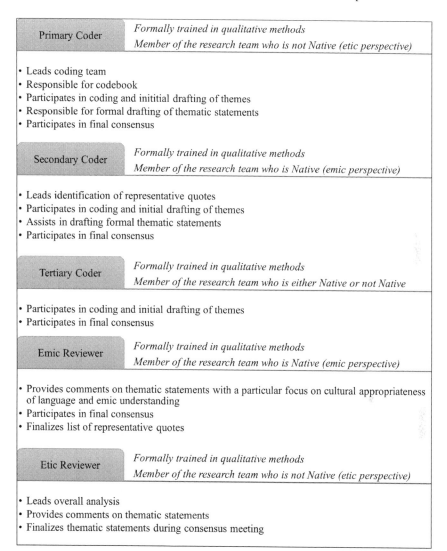

Primary Coder	*Formally trained in qualitative methods* *Member of the research team who is not Native (etic perspective)*

- Leads coding team
- Responsible for codebook
- Participates in coding and inititial drafting of themes
- Responsible for formal drafting of thematic statements
- Participates in final consensus

Secondary Coder	*Formally trained in qualitative methods* *Member of the research team who is Native (emic perspective)*

- Leads identification of representative quotes
- Participates in coding and initial drafting of themes
- Assists in drafting formal thematic statements
- Participates in final consensus

Tertiary Coder	*Formally trained in qualitative methods* *Member of the research team who is either Native or not Native*

- Participates in coding and initial drafting of themes
- Participates in final consensus

Emic Reviewer	*Formally trained in qualitative methods* *Member of the research team who is Native (emic perspective)*

- Provides comments on thematic statements with a particular focus on cultural appropriateness of language and emic understanding
- Participates in final consensus
- Finalizes list of representative quotes

Etic Reviewer	*Formally trained in qualitative methods* *Member of the research team who is not Native (etic perspective)*

- Leads overall analysis
- Provides comments on thematic statements
- Finalizes thematic statements during consensus meeting

Figure 1.3.   Roles of Qualitative Analysts. *Credit*: Christine M. Daley.

coder led this process. The thematic statements were then given to the two reviewers, also formally trained in qualitative methods and providing different viewpoints (emic and etic). The reviewers suggested modifications to the thematic statements, and then the group of five met to finalize the themes and ensure they were representative of the data. The emic reviewer was responsible for review of representative quotes. We followed this analysis procedure for each stratum, then looked across them to understand how similar or different the strata were.

To code the data for quantitative content analysis, we again selected coders, this time identifying two individuals to use a set of numeric codes to code the data, including one emic and one etic perspective for each culture area. There was some overlap among coders for the quantitative coding and coders for the qualitative coding, but not the entire team, largely because the different analyses were done at different time points. A new codebook was developed with codes specific to the types of analyses that we wanted to complete across survey and interview data. Specifically, we were interested in the preferred term used to describe Native people, whom or what participants cited as their primary influences on their identity, positive and negative views of religion and spirituality, types of religion represented among participants, feelings about CDIB (Certificate of Degree of Indian Blood) cards, and reasons behind feelings about CDIB cards. We created codes inductively and then used them to code all transcripts a second time. Discrepancies among coders led to discussions to ensure 100 percent inter-coder reliability.

We combined our spreadsheets of survey data and quantitative interview data for analysis in SAS software. We ran basic frequencies for all data and then collapsed some categories within demographic variables to allow for easier analysis. We then ran frequencies by each of several collapsed demographic variables, including the following:

- Gender (male, female)
- Age (18–29, 30–49, 50+)
- Marital status (married or in a relationship versus not married or in a relationship)
- Children (yes, no)
- Education level (GED or high school, post-high school training or two-year college degree, four-year college degree or higher)
- Employment status (yes, no)
- American Indian along versus in combination with another race/ethnicity
- Tribal enrollment status (yes, no)
- Area where raised (reservation or tribal trust land versus urban, suburban, or rural off-reservation)
- Culture area (California; Great Basin & Plateau; Great Lakes; Northeast and Southeast; Northern Plains; Northwest Coast, Arctic, and Subarctic; Southern Plains; Southwest)

For the purposes of this text, we did not conduct high-level analyses, such as regression modeling or hypothesis testing. We decided that the most important information in these interviews and surveys was tied to the words of our participants. We did not want to reduce their views on their own identities to a p-value or any other statistical measure.

Native 24/7 Participants

Approximately 9.7 million people in the United States identified themselves as American Indian or Alaska Native on the 2020 US Census; this is 2.9 percent of the US population. Of that, nearly 3.7 million individuals identified as solely American Indian or Alaska Native while the other over 5.9 million identified as American Indian or Alaska Native in combination with one or more races/ethnicities (US Census Bureau 2021). These numbers represent an 85 percent increase in American Indian and Alaska Native people since 2010, including a 27 percent increase in those individuals claiming only Native ancestry and a 160 percent increase in those claiming mixed ancestry. The greatest increases in population are seen in the Midwestern and Southern states, with the overall greatest increase in Tennessee at 194 percent. Every state in the United States, as well as the District of Columbia and Puerto Rico, showed increases in numbers of Native peoples between 2010 and 2020. These numbers likely represent a combination of increased birth rates and decreased mortality rates in Native communities and an increased willingness of people to self-identify as American Indian or Alaska Native. *Native 24/7* was conducted during the first half of this time period, between 2011 and 2015, during what appears to be a population explosion or, at the very least, an explosion of individuals willing to identify themselves as American Indian or Alaska Native.

Seven-hundred and thirty-four individuals participated in *Native 24/7*, including 636 who completed some or all of the survey questions and 624 who completed the interviews. Five-hundred and twenty-eight participants completed both the interview and the survey. Participant demographic characteristics are listed in table 1.2.

Though we planned for one-half of our participants to be male and one-half to be female, we had significantly greater participation among females (61%). This is not uncommon. In our experience, women seem to be more willing to participate in research, at least the type of research we do. We initially included a third gender category for individuals to self-identify; we had only one participant indicate a third gender, listing "Two Spirit." The term "Two Spirit" was first coined in 1990 in Winnipeg, Canada, as an umbrella term for many third genders in numerous Indigenous communities in the Americas. Two Spirit is not the same as gay or transgender; rather, it is

Table 1.2. Native 24/7 Participant Demographics

Demographic Characteristic	N (%)
Gender (N=734)	
Male	284 (39%)
Female	449 (61%)
Two Spirit	1 (<1%)
Age (N=734)	
18-29	249 (34%)
30-49	269 (37%)
50+	216 (29%)
Marital Status	
Married or in a Relationship	323 (53%)
Never Married, Divorced, Separated, or Widowed	282 (47%)
Children (N=621)	
Yes	416 (67%)
No	205 (33%)
Education Level (N=623)	
GED or High School	167 (27%)
Post-High School Training or 2-year College Degree	264 (42%)
4-year College Degree or Higher	192 (31%)
Employment (N=617)	
Yes	423 (69%)
No	194 (31%)
American Indian Alone or Mixed Race (N=636)	
American Indian	498 (78%)
American Indian in Combination with Another Race/Ethnicity	138 (22%)
Enrollment Status (N=620)	
Enrolled	509 (82%)
Not Enrolled	111 (18%)
Area Where Raised (N=625)	
Reservation or Tribal Trust Land	329 (53%)
Off-Reservation	296 (47%)
Culture Area (N=734)	
California	52 (7%)
Great Basin & Plateau	66 (9%)
Great Lakes	128 (17%)
Northeast & Southeast	70 (10%)
Northern Plains	136 (19%)
Northwest Coast, Arctic, Subarctic	45 (6%)
Southern Plains	139 (19%)
Southwest	98 (13%)

Notes: Percentages may not add up to 100 due to rounding; percentages are presented as column percentages. Not all participants answered all questions; the appropriate N for each question is listed.

Credit: Christine M. Daley, Charley Lewis, and Joseph Pacheco[1]

about two genders residing within one person (Enos 2017). It is a Native-specific term not used by other racial or ethnic groups and refers to people who follow traditional roles in particular Indigenous Nations. The role of a Two Spirit individual in many Nations includes a spiritual responsibility and often a role as a keeper of balance and/or healer of a particular type. Examples of different types of Two Spirit individuals can be found throughout history in many different Nations, but all acknowledge the continuum of gender identity and expression. We did not include a third gender in our analyses because it would have potentially identified the single individual who identified as such.

The age distribution of *Native 24/7* participants was guided by our sampling frame that was stratified into three age groups. We had a slight overrepresentation of people aged 30–49 (37%) and a slight underrepresentation of people aged 50+ (29%). *Native 24/7* participants were weighted toward people with children (67%) and people who were married (53%). Participants were also more highly educated than the national average, with 31 percent of *Native 24/7* participants holding a bachelor's degree or higher versus 16 percent nationally (PNPI 2020). The unemployment rate of *Native 24/7* participants was 31 percent, likely related to a high number of college students and other young people participating and to a large number of participants from reservations or tribal trust land (53%), which tend to have higher unemployment rates. We had planned for inclusion of similar numbers of individuals from reservation, non-reservation urban, and non-reservation rural communities. We wound up with over half of our participants from reservation or tribal trust communities. Because of that, we combined all non-reservation communities for the purpose of quantitative analyses. Qualitative analysis included all three different types of communities.

Participants were more likely to be American Indian alone (78%) rather than in combination with another race or ethnicity. This is a much higher proportion of individuals claiming only Native ancestry rather than mixed heritage compared to the overall population, in which 66 percent of individuals are of mixed heritage. Participants who were of mixed heritage were asked to list their other racial or ethnic group or groups. Of the 22 percent of participants who claimed mixed ancestry, the majority listed White (57%), followed by Latino (24%), Black or African American (10%), Hawaiian or other Pacific Islander (4%), and Asian (3%). It is possible that people who participated in this study about Native identity were more likely to only claim their Native ancestry because of the topic being discussed. It is likewise possible that more people with only Native ancestry were interested in this type of study. It is also possible that the high percentage of individuals claiming only American Indian or Alaska Native heritage has to do with the culture areas from which we recruited. Some culture areas were over-represented, including most notably the Southern Plains (19%), Northern Plains (19%), and Great Lakes (17%) areas, as well as the Southwest (13%). This is likely due to our location in the Central Plains and large recruitment events we attended in the Great Lakes and Southwest. Those regions tend to have lower percentages of individuals who claim mixed heritage.

Not all participants were willing to list their tribal affiliation on the de-mographic survey; 508 participants named one or more tribal affiliations. The reasons for not listing a tribal affiliation are unknown (we did not ask) but could include individuals who did not know their affiliation, as well as those who did not wish to say for some reason. Of the individuals who named a tribe, 421 (83%) named one tribe and 87 (17%) named multiple tribes. There were 121 different tribal nations represented by all participants. The single tribe named most often was Navajo, with 64 individuals (13%) claiming this affiliation, including 52 people who identified as Navajo alone, 3 people who identified as *Diné* alone (the word for Navajo in their own lan-guage), and 9 people who identified as Navajo in combination with one or more other tribes. To better understand who the participants were, we com-bined tribal nations who sometimes refer to themselves as a group (e.g., the Sioux Confederacy, the Iroquois or *Haudenosaunee* Confederacy, or the *An-ishinaabe* tribes). The most commonly named tribal affiliation was some type of Anishinaabe tribe, including people identifying as any of the Chippewa, Ojibwe, Odawa, or Potawatomi peoples, as well a few other smaller groups. One hundred-thirty-three individuals affiliated with one of the Anishinaabe tribes (26%), including 109 who named only an Anishinaabe tribe and 24 who named Anishinaabe plus at least one other tribe. The second most commonly named affiliation was the Sioux Confederacy, which included individuals identifying as some type of Lakota, Dakota, or Nakota people. A total of 67 people (13%) claimed one of the Sioux tribes, including 56 who named only a Sioux tribe and 11 who named a Sioux tribe in combination with one or more additional tribes. Participants were asked separately if they were enrolled in a tribe; 82 percent said that they were enrolled.

Cultural Connectedness

One piece of identity that we attempted to understand was connection to culture. Throughout the following chapters we will explore connections to various Native cultures through the words of *Native 24/7* participants. We asked some questions in the demographic survey in an effort to understand cultural connectedness and factors that might be related to cultural connectedness as well. We examined race/ethnicity of each parent, as well as spouse or significant other and friends, Indigenous language fluency, participation in traditional activities and living in traditional ways, and the importance of maintenance of Native identity (see table 1.1 for questions).

The majority of participants said that both of their parents were Native (66%); among those who reported only one Native parent, it was more likely to be their mother than their father (19% versus 12%). Few participants had no Native parents (4%); this is likely individuals who were adopted. Participants were more likely to have a spouse or significant other who was also Native (52%); however, friends tended to be both Native and non-Native (see figure 1.4).

The majority of participants had some level of familiarity with their tribe's language, though levels of fluency varied. The majority of participants believed they could speak their tribal language a little, but not well (51%). Only 8 percent said they could speak their language well and 13 percent said moderately well, leaving 28 percent of participants saying they could not speak their language at all. This is similar to a 2014 report in *Indian Country Today* that stated that a Native North American language is spoken in about 15 percent of homes where the residents identified as solely American

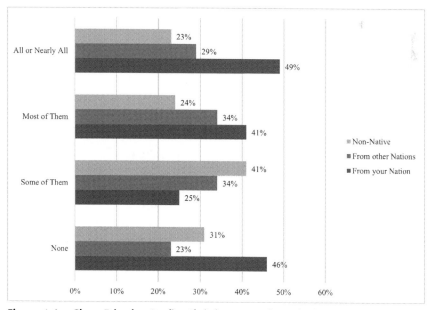

Figure 1.4. Close Friends. *Credit*: **Christine M. Daley, Charley Lewis, and Joseph Pacheco.**

Indian or Alaska Native (Lee 2018). According to the Endangered Languages Project, there are about 160 Native North American languages still spoken in the United States. All but one of them are classified as "endangered," "severely endangered," or "dormant." The only language not classified as such is Navajo, which is classified "at risk" (Endangered Languages Project 2021). Although there are 171,000 fluent speakers of the Navajo language, making it the most commonly spoken Native North American language, there has been a significant drop in speakers over the past several decades. In 1980, about 93 percent of Navajos spoke the language; in 2010 it was down to 51 percent (Denetclaw 2017).

Overall, participants stated that they felt that they lived their lives following a Native way of life, however they personally defined it. Forty percent of participants said they lived in a Native way "a lot," and an additional 44 percent said they sometimes live in a Native way, leaving only 16 percent following a Native way of life rarely or not at all. However, they also felt that they lived their lives sometimes following a non-Native way of life, with 49 percent saying sometimes and 29 percent saying a lot, and 22 percent saying rarely or not at all. Therefore, the majority of participants felt as though they live in both Native and non-Native worlds. When asked about participation in traditional activities, the vast majority of participants (94%) participated in at least some of their own culture's traditions. Eighty-one percent participated in traditional activities of another Native culture, and 85 percent participated in traditional activities from a non-Native culture. Participants were more likely to participate in traditional activities from their own Native culture more often and least likely to participate in non-Native traditional activities often (see fgure 1.5). Participation in traditional activities clearly echoes participants' beliefs about leading both Native and non-Native ways of life.

Lastly, participants were asked about the importance they place on their personal and family maintenance of Native and non-Native values and practices. Answers to these questions mirrored the other questions, with an importance placed on maintaining multiple identities and values, though a preference for their own Nations' values and practices. Eighty percent of participants said that it was very important for them to personally maintain their own Native Nation's values and practices; an additional 16 percent said that it was somewhat important. When asked about other Nations' values and practices, 75 percent said it was somewhat or very important. Fifty percent said it was somewhat or very important to maintain non-Native values and practices. Participants placed somewhat more importance on their own maintenance of values and practices as opposed to family members main-

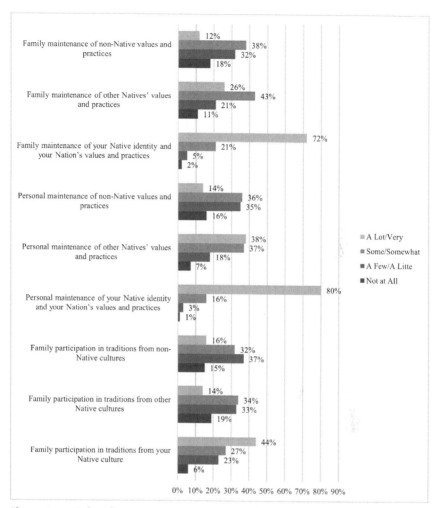

Figure 1.5. **Cultural Connectedness Questions.** *Credit*: Christine M. Daley, Charley Lewis, and Joseph Pacheco.

tenance, with 91 percent saying that it was very or somewhat important to them that their family members maintained their Nations' values and practices. Similar trends were seen for family maintenance of other Nations' and non-Native values and practices.

Participant views of these simple questions about cultural connectedness provide a glimpse into the pages that follow, which focus primarily on what *Native 24/7* participants said in their interviews. We focus on the words of participants to present their views as clearly as possible. In chapter 2, participants tell us about the terms that they would prefer others use to describe their racial or ethnic category. Chapter 3 delves into participants' thoughts on culture, history, and heritage, and the roles they play in contemporary Native identity. Chapter 4 explores the connections among family, community, and relationships and identity. Chapter 5 investigates religion and spirituality and their connections to modern Native identity. Chapter 6 looks at participants' views of Certificate of Degree of Indian Blood Cards and tribal enrollment. Finally, chapter 7 attempts to provide some type of conclusion about what it means to be American Indian/Native American/Indian/Native/Indigenous/insert tribal name/etc., in contemporary America.

Note

1. Charley Lewis and Joseph Pacheco provided statistical analysis that was integral to the writing of this book.

CHAPTER TWO

~

"So, What Should I Call You?
Indian? Native? Something Else?"

Preferences for Terminology

The day had come for the championship game in the all-Native basketball tournament. Many teams had played valiantly, but on the last day the competition came down to the highly competitive Lakota and Navajo teams. The tension was high as all waited to see which would be the best team.

Prior to the game, some of the Lakota players went to watch the Navajos practice. They were awed and somewhat intimidated by the Navajos' impressive display of skills. One Lakota who was particularly anxious and insecure pointed out to his teammates that some of the Navajo players had facial hair. "Everyone knows that Indians don't have facial hair," he stated. Another Lakota added that some of the Navajos also had suspiciously dark skin. They concluded, disdainfully, that clearly these were not Native people and, in fact, were probably a "bunch of Mexicans." The so-called Navajos should be disqualified from the tournament, leaving the Lakota team the winner by default.

That same afternoon, some Navajo players went to watch the Lakota team practice. The Lakotas had a lot of skillful moves that made the Navajos worry. One Navajo observed, "That guy's skin sure looks awful light." Another added, "Yeah, and most of them have short hair." They concluded, disdainfully, that clearly these were not Native people and, in fact, were probably a "bunch of white guys." The so-called Lakotas should be disqualified from the tournament, leaving the Navajos the winners by default.

The captains from both teams brought their accusations to the referee just before the game. Both teams agreed that Native identity must be established before the game could be played and that whichever team could not establish Native identity to everyone's satisfaction must forfeit. The Lakota captain suggested that everyone show his tribal enrollment card as proof of identity. The Lakotas promptly displayed their "red cards," but some of the Navajos did not have enrollment cards. The Lakotas were ready to celebrate their victory when the Navajo captain protested that carrying an enrollment card was a product of colonization and not an indicator of true identity. He suggested that real proof would be a display of indigenous language skills, and each Navajo proceeded to recite his clan affiliations in the traditional way of introducing himself in the Navajo language. Some of the Lakotas were able to speak their language, but others were not. The teams went back and forth proposing standards of proof of identity, but each proposed standard was self-serving and could not be met by the other team. As the sun began to set, the frustrated referees canceled the championship game. Because of accusations and disagreements that could not be resolved there would be no champion in the indigenous tournament.

The above story has been told and printed many times; this version comes from Weaver's 2001 article, "Indigenous Identity: What Is It, and Who Really Has It?" Regardless of the telling, and the minor variations, the main crux of the story remains unchanged—American Indian identity is complex and difficult to navigate, even among Native peoples themselves. As noted by Weaver (2001), "Indigenous identity is a truly complex and somewhat controversial topic. There is little agreement on precisely what constitutes an Indigenous identity, how to measure it, and who truly has it (240). Pewewardy (2003) echoes this when he states,

> An ongoing saga of defining 'who's an Indian' continues into another millennium as does the sociopolitical meaning of the phrase. Indigenous peoples are subjected to many political definitions even within their own dynamic levels of tribal politics as well as by states and the federal government. The conflicting policies of tribal government acknowledgment, federal government blood quantum criteria, and a myriad of self-identifications contribute to this paradox of cultural identity. (73)

Additionally, many people, Native and non-Native, view "Indian" identity as a colonially imposed concept since the concept of an "Indian" did not exist until contact with Europeans.

Furthermore, those who work with Indian peoples and in Native communities know that there is no "one" way Indian peoples look, contrary to the stereotypes proliferated by settlers and descendants since the beginnings of European colonization of the Americas. There is no one true American Indian phenotypical appearance or presentation. Indians have a variety of skin colors, heights, weights, hair colors, nose shapes, and eye shapes. Mihesuah (1998) noted:

> Not all individuals claiming to be Indian "look Indian," nor were many born into tribal environments. Many are not tribally enrolled and others who claim to be Indian are not Indian at all. Some Indians who appear Caucasian or Black go back and forth assuming Indian, white, and Black identities, while others who have lived most of their lives as non-Indians decide to "become Indians" at a later age. Some individuals are Indian by virtue of biological connection, but know little about their cultural mores either because of a lack of interest; because there was no one to teach them; or because it was not (or is not) socially or economically profitable to pursue an Indian identity due to the time period, location, and degree of racism, prejudice, and stereotypes . . . Because of assimilation, acculturation, intermarriage with non-Indians, American Indians have a variety of references to describe themselves: full-blood, traditional, mixed-blood, cross-blood, half-breed, progressive, enrolled, unenrolled, re-Indianized, multi-heritage, bicultural, post-Indian, or simply, "I'm _____ (tribal affiliation)." (193–194).

Despite questions about the continued value of identity as a category for social scientists (Brubaker and Cooper 2000), it remains an important focus in the public and academic consciousness (Ehala 2018). Its applications have been used to understand a nearly never-ending stream of circumstances including social justice activism, cultural revival, and ethnic stratification, to name a few examples (Soto-Márquez 2019; Castells 2011; Escobar 2008; Polletta and Jasper 2001). However, as some Indigenous scholars have noted, for Indigenous peoples around the world, the importance of identity constructions goes beyond theoretical concerns. Rather, it more importantly functions as one way to support sovereignty and self-determination, designations at the foundations of many contemporary issues in these communities (Adese, Todd, and Stevenson 2017; Grande, San Pedro, and Windchief 2015; Alfred and Corntassel 2005; Corntassel 2003; Grande 2000).

To understand Indigenous identities and experiences, one must first recognize that the Indigenous experience is inherently political (Schmidt 2011; Corntassel 2003). Defined externally by governments and intergovernmental organizations, such as the United Nations, Indigenous peoples are often bound by external definitions of what it means to be Indigenous in order to receive recognition (Corntassel 2003; Alfred and Corntassel 2005;

Garroutte 2003). This dynamic has proven to be particularly harmful as groups struggle to identify themselves in internally meaningful ways while also being shaped by governmental and international narratives, thus leading to a crisis of "authenticity" (Conklin 1997). This struggle is particularly true in the United States where the racialized status of American Indian communities is unique among American minority groups. Using a "logic of elimination," which constructs "Nativeness" on an ever-decreasing scale aimed at total erasure, individuals are measured based upon the amount of "Indian blood" that they possess (Wolfe 2006). This serves as the basis for federal recognition as a member of a federally recognized tribal nation (Spruhan 2018).[1] These circumstances have left indelible marks on the internal dynamics of these communities through internalized oppression that often manifests as exclusionary opinions and practices toward people of mixed ancestry (Weaver 2001). This classification is in direct contrast to Black racialization, for example, which has historically relied upon the "one-drop-rule" which labels an individual possessing any amount of Black ancestry as Black (Wolfe 2006; Davis 2010).

In the United States, the legacy of settler-colonialism hangs heavy over conceptions of what it means to be "American Indian." The history of federal Indian policy can be understood as a project of defining who qualifies to be American Indian (Garroutte 2003; Mann 2004). Due to this legacy, Indigenous self-determination is of critical importance politically and culturally, ensuring that conversations around the appropriateness of terms such as "American Indian," "Native American," and other similar combinations are not going away anytime soon.

According to Yellow Bird (1999), "The labels 'Indian,' 'American Indian,' and 'Native American' have been criticized in academic scholarship. I have suggested that these names are oppressive, counterfeit identities that are misleading, inaccurate, and used to control and subjugate the identities of Indigenous Peoples and undermine their right to use tribal affiliation as a preeminent national identity" (86).

Recognizing the importance of terminology to conceptions of individual and collective identity, participant preference for particular terms to identify themselves served as a framework throughout *Native 24/7* interviews. At the start of the interview, participants were asked, "Do you prefer a particular term to describe your ethnicity?" The term preferred by the participant was then used by the interviewer for the entirety of their discussion. For example, if a participant referred to himself or herself as Native, then he or she would be referred to as Native throughout the remainder of the interview. If a participant identified as Lakota, then he or she would be referred to as Lakota for the rest of the interview. As would be expected, there was no singular agreement among participants; instead, they used a variety of all-encompassing collective terms in addition to more community or tribal specific terms. In total, participants used 755 terms to identify themselves. The reasons for this were as varied as the terms themselves. Some participants even preferred a combination of terms; they used a collective term, such as Native American, in addition to their tribal name. In his 1999 study on preferred terms employed by Native peoples, Yellow Bird (1999) found that:

> The diversity of labels chosen by the respondents and their reasons for choosing them demonstrate that there are numerous opinions about the terms used to identify First Nations Peoples. While certain labels are regarded as more appropriate or desirable by some of the respondents, others see these same labels as oppressive, confusing, or exclusive. It is clear, however, that respondents are not using their preferred labels in a purely reflexive manner and instead use them in a critically calculated way to resist or counter what they see as inherent problems with other labels. In addition, several use different labels interchangeably, suggesting active efforts to define and be respectful of the complex identities and situations of Indigenous Peoples. (15)

Of the collective terminology preferred by participants, including American Indian, Indian, Native American, Native, and Indigenous, there was a clear preference for the term "Native American" as the predominant collective term for the Indigenous peoples of North America. Two-hundred and eighty-two participants (43%) stated they preferred "Native American." Participants provided a number of reasons for this preference (see figure 2.1). One participant, a twenty-two-year-old male from a Northeast reservation community, stated he preferred Native American because "like Dad always said, Indians are from India, so, we're Natives." Second to Native American was "American Indian," preferred by 82 participants (14%).

Other collective terms used by *Native 24/7* participants included Native, Indian, Alaska Native, First Nation, Native American Indian, North American Indian, First American, Indigenous, American Native, Native Indian, and Aboriginal.

One fifty-three-year-old male participant from a California reservation community stated that he preferred 'skin and 'jun (short for Redskin and Injun, respectively). He stated that "in the area where I'm at, it's either 'skin or 'jun. . . . Guys will come up and go, 'What's up 'skin?' or 'What up, 'jun?', like Injun . . . I know a lot of people don't like 'Native American' . . . because a lot of White people . . . say they're native American. They don't mean 'American Indian', they just mean they are native to America."

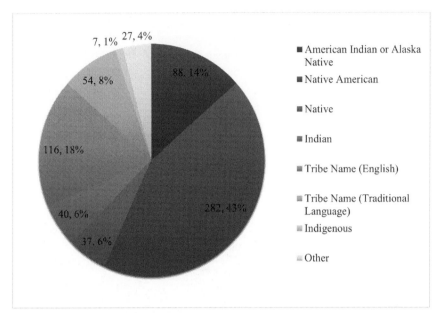

Figure 2.1. Preferred Terminology (N=651). *Credit:* **Christine M. Daley, Charley Lewis, and Joseph Pacheco.**

Some participants (N=170, 26%) stated that they preferred to use their tribal name as opposed to an overarching term. Among these participants, the most named tribal nation was the Navajo Nation with 38 individuals, including 20 participants who identified as Diné (the word used to designate the people of that Nation in their own language) and 18 as Navajo. Second to Diné/Navajo was Anishinaabe with 25 participants identifying as Anishinaabe or one of the tribes comprising the Anishinaabe, such as Potawatomi or Ojibwe. Third was Sioux with 20 participants claiming that as their affiliation. As with the Anishinaabe, this included those who identified with several different tribes, including Lakota, Dakota, and Nakota, and various bands within those categories. A total of 83 tribes or tribal nations were claimed by *Native 24/7* participants. Within this, more specific identifiers were often preferred to describe tribal affiliations. These included names drawn from participants' own tribal languages, such as Diné in Navajo, or externally imposed names that have been adopted by tribal members, such as Cherokee, originally a Creek word for "people with another language."

When compared to participant answers on the demographic surveys (see chapter 1), a similar picture emerges, with Navajo as the individual nation represented the most and Anishinaabe and Sioux as the groupings of tribes represented the most. However, more Navajos preferred to be called by their tribal affiliation overall than any of the groupings of tribes. On the survey, 13 percent of all participants claimed Navajo, whereas 26 percent claimed Anishinaabe and 13 percent claimed Sioux. When asked in an interview the preferred term to use, the majority of Anishinaabe and Sioux participants preferred one of the other, more generic, terms for Native people (81% and 70%, respectively). Among Navajo participants, 59 percent preferred to be identified as Navajo or Diné rather than one of the more generic terms. In addition, only 3 participants listed Diné on the survey, but 20 used it as the term they preferred as an identifier. This difference may be an effect of the context of writing something down on a survey versus talking to someone, specifically another Native person.

Many participants mentioned preferring or using multiple identifiers, specifically based on context. For example, a twenty-six-year-old woman who grew up in an urban area in the Northeast explained, "I generally refer to myself by the name of my tribe, but then with non-Natives, some find that confusing because they don't know individual tribes, and so, I just refer to myself as Native or Native American." This sentiment was echoed by many other participants who also felt the need to use a more generic term among non-Natives and a more specific term referring to their tribe when among other Natives. Interviewers for Native 24/7 were primarily Native, with only a few exceptions when there was a time problem during large event recruitment. It is also possible that there were differences based on whether the interviewer was from the same tribe as the interviewee; we did not examine this aspect, but it would not have accounted for many individual answers.

There was a small subset of participants, 30, who stated that they had no preference for one term over another as long as that term was used respectfully. One participant simply stated that no label should ever be used when identifying a human being; however, he did not indicate what should be used instead of a label. Table 2.1 presents preferences for terminology based on participant demographic factors.

The question of what term to use was an open-ended one. In other words, participants could answer whatever they liked in a spontaneous way. Because of this, it is not clear if certain terms would be preferred above others if all terms were listed. For example, if all participants were asked to choose from only "American Indian" or "Native American," there would be a clearer picture of preference between the two terms. The intent of the question, however, was to determine a preferred way to be addressed rather than to delineate a ranked preference of terms. Nonetheless, there were clear trends in the overall sample, as discussed above, as well as trends based on different

Table 2.1. Preferred Terminology of Participants by Demographic Characteristics

Demographic Characteristic	American Indian or Alaska Native N (%)	Native American N (%)	Native N (%)	Indian N (%)	Tribe Name (English) N (%)	Tribe Name (Traditional Language) N (%)	Indigenous N (%)	Other N (%)
Gender (N=651)								
Male	33 (38%)	98 (35%)	18 (48%)	19 (48%)	50 (43%)	23 (43%)	4 (57%)	16 (59%)
Female	55 (63%)	184 (65%)	19 (51%)	21 (53%)	66 (57%)	31 (57%)	3 (43%)	11 (41%)
Age (N=651)								
18-29	31 (35%)	118 (42%)	19 (51%)	11 (28%)	29 (25%)	13 (24%)	1 (14%)	5 (19%)
30-49	28 (32%)	99 (35%)	11 (30%)	18 (45%)	42 (36%)	24 (44%)	3 (43%)	9 (33%)
50+	29 (33%)	65 (23%)	7 (19%)	11 (28%)	45 (39%)	17 (31%)	3 (43%)	13 (48%)
Marital Status (N=561)								
Married/In a Relationship	34 (49%)	112 (48%)	16 (44%)	21 (60%)	54 (62%)	27 (59%)	5 (71%)	11 (42%)
Never Married/Divorced/Separated/Widowed	36 (51%)	119 (52%)	20 (56%)	14 (40%)	33 (38%)	19 (41%)	2 (29%)	15 (58%)
Children (N=550)								
Yes	43 (61%)	155 (65%)	17 (47%)	28 (78%)	63 (68%)	31 (69%)	6 (86%)	15 (60%)
No	27 (39%)	84 (35%)	19 (53%)	8 (22%)	29 (32%)	14 (31%)	1 (14%)	10 (40%)
Education Level (N=550)								
GED or High School	23 (33%)	70 (29%)	11 (31%)	4 (11%)	17 (19%)	11 (24%)	1 (14%)	5 (20%)
Post-High School Training or 2-year College Degree	26 (37%)	111 (46%)	19 (53%)	18 (50%)	38 (42%)	20 (43%)	2 (29%)	13 (52%)
4-year College Degree or Higher	21 (30%)	58 (24%)	6 (17%)	14 (39%)	36 (40%)	15 (33%)	4 (57%)	7 (28%)
Employment Status (N=615)								
Currently Employed	50 (71%)	170 (71%)	26 (74%)	27 (75%)	66 (73%)	32 (71%)	5 (71%)	16 (64%)
Not Currently Employed	20 (29%)	69 (29%)	9 (26%)	9 (25%)	25 (27%)	13 (29%)	2 (29%)	9 (36%)

American Indian Alone or Mixed Race (N=560)								
American Indian	63 (86%)	193 (79%)	28 (78%)	24 (67%)	65 (70%)	39 (83%)	5 (71%)	10 (40%)
American Indian in Combination with Another Race/Ethnicity	10 (14%)	50 (21%)	8 (22%)	12 (33%)	28 (30%)	8 (17%)	2 (29%)	15 (60%)
Enrollment Status (N=546)								
Enrolled	62 (91%)	198 (84%)	31 (86%)	29 (81%)	72 (79%)	36 (77%)	6 (86%)	15 (60%)
Not Enrolled	6 (9%)	38 (16%)	5 (14%)	7 (19%)	19 (21%)	11 (23%)	1 (14%)	10 (40%)
Area Where Raised (N=552)								
Reservation or Tribal Trust Land	41 (58%)	124 (52%)	17 (47%)	19 (53%)	43 (47%)	33 (72%)	5 (71%)	10 (40%)
Off-Reservation	30 (42%)	116 (48%)	19 (53%)	17 (47%)	48 (53%)	13 (28%)	2 (29%)	15 (60%)
Culture Area (N=651)								
California	4 (5%)	21 (7%)	4 (11%)	5 (13%)	8 (7%)	1 (2%)	0 (0%)	2 (7%)
Great Basin & Plateau	10 (11%)	29 (10%)	0 (0%)	5 (13%)	15 (13%)	2 (4%)	0 (0%)	2 (7%)
Great Lakes	4 (5%)	49 (17%)	12 (32%)	8 (20%)	16 (14%)	7 (13%)	2 (29%)	10 (37%)
Northeast & Southeast	13 (15%)	26 (9%)	4 (11%)	7 (18%)	11 (9%)	2 (4%)	0 (0%)	3 (11%)
Northern Plains	10 (11%)	60 (21%)	6 (16%)	3 (8%)	14 (12%)	8 (15%)	1 (14%)	4 (15%)
Northwest Coast, Arctic, Subarctic	16 (18%)	7 (2%)	1 (3%)	3 (8%)	4 (3%)	9 (17%)	0 (0%)	1 (4%)
Southern Plains	22 (25%)	48 (17%)	9 (24%)	9 (23%)	30 (26%)	9 (17%)	4 (57%)	3 (11%)
Southwest	9 (10%)	42 (15%)	1 (3%)	0 (0%)	18 (16%)	16 (30%)	0 (0%)	2 (7%)

NOTE: Total N for each demographic variable are different based on whether or not an individual answered the demographic question. Percentages are presented as column percentages. Percentages have been rounded to the nearest whole number. Percentages may not total 100 due to rounding.

Credit: Christine M. Daley, Charley Lewis, and Joseph Pacheco

demographic factors. Because many terms were used by few people overall, it is difficult to interpret trends for those terms. The more often named descriptors, including American Indian, Native American, Native, Indian, and the use of a tribal name in general in either English or a Native language can be examined for trends that may provide some information about the things that influence an individual's choice of the term (see table 2.1). It should be noted, however, that, in some cases the numbers are so low for a given term that interpreting a trend is impossible. For example, only seven individuals used the term "Indigenous."

Gender did not appear to have a large influence on preferred terminology, though men were somewhat more likely to use the shortened, "Native" or "Indian," rather than "American Indian/Alaska Native" or "Native American." Age appeared to have some influence on views, not unexpectedly, given that different terms have been preferred over the last several decades, similar to the way terms for people of African heritage have changed over time. In this group of people, individuals in the lowest age range (18–29 years) were more likely to prefer "Native American" and those in the oldest age range (50+ years) were more likely to prefer "American Indian." Those in the middle age range (30–49 years) were split between these terms, but were a bit more likely to prefer "Indian" or a tribal name in their traditional language. People in the oldest age range were more likely to prefer a tribal name in English and were the least likely to prefer the shortened "Indian" or "Native." It is likely that the use of "American Indian" trending to "Native American" as the age groups lower is due to changing use of the terms over the past few decades. The use of a tribal name in English by older individuals could be an effect of the boarding school era, during which use of traditional language resulted in often cruel punishments.

Having children did not have a large effect on the preferred term, though there is a trend toward a preference of a tribal name in either English or a traditional language, potentially showing parents' desire to instill tribal pride in their children through using the name. Parents were also somewhat more likely to use the term "Indian" and somewhat less likely to use the term "Native." Marital status also had little effect, with a slight tendency of people who were married or in a relationship having a preference for either "Indian" or a tribal name. Employment status appeared to have no effect on preference.

Education level had a somewhat clearer effect on preferred term. Individuals with less formal education (high school or GED) were more likely to prefer the term "American Indian" and less likely to use a tribal name. People with a four-year college degree or graduate degree of some type preferred a tribal name, more likely in English, or use of the simplified "Indian," which was a preference of very few people with little formal education. They also had more of a preference for "American Indian" rather than "Native American." People with some post-high school training or a two-year college degree had a stronger preference for "Native American" or either of the shortened terms ("Native" or "Indian"). It is clear that some post-high school education has a different effect on preferred term than continued formal education, but the reasons behind this are unknown in this study. A closer examination of how Native people are described in formal education is warranted to understand the changing preference for term. It may also be tied to the field of study of individuals in *Native 24/7*. It is possible and likely that different fields of study use different terms. If, for example, people with higher levels of formal education in this study had degrees in American Indian Studies, that could explain their preference for the term "American Indian" or their preference for a tribal name.

Participants who claimed only Native heritage were more likely to use the terms "American Indian" or "Native American" than those who claimed mixed heritage, who preferred "Indian" or "Native." Those who claimed mixed heritage were less likely to use a tribal name in a tribal language. Enrollment status seemed to have little effect on preferred term, other than a slight preference for "American Indian."

Native 24/7 participants were asked where they grew up in two ways, including geographic region of the country and whether or not they grew up on a reservation or tribal trust land. There were clear trends in term preference by both of these factors. Individuals who grew up in reservation or tribal trust land communities were more likely to prefer "American Indian" or "Native American" over "Indian" or "Native"; those who grew up off-reservation or tribal trust land were exactly opposite. Individuals who grew up on reservations or tribal trust land were far more likely to use a traditional language if they preferred the name of their tribe; those who grew up off-reservation or tribal trust land were more likely to use the English name for their tribe. It is probable people growing up on reservations would be more likely to hear their tribal language or see it written around them, likely influencing how they would talk about their tribes. The preference for a more formal term rather than a shortened version has less clear reasons behind it, but could reflect a shortened vernacular in urban areas that is less common in tribal communities.

There were clear regional preferences in terminology. The use of a traditional language for tribal name was preferred in the Southwest and the Northwest Coast, Arctic, and Subarctic regions. These are areas with a large number of speakers (including monolingual speakers of Native languages) and where many times traditional languages are used as signage and in tribal documents. The use of a tribal language may also indicate people who speak that language or have a significant number of family members who speak that language. Californians and people from the Great Lakes area were more likely to prefer the shortened "Indian" or "Native," with a stronger preference for "Native" in the Great Lakes. Preferences in the Northeast and Southeast trended toward "American Indian" or "Indian." The strongest preference in the Northern Plains was for "Native American," though that region had a heterogeneous response. There was a likewise heterogeneous response in the Southern Plains with similar preferences for "American Indian," "Indian," "Native," and a tribal name in English. Participants from the Great Basin and Plateau area were also heterogeneous in their response, with little preference other than a lack of using a tribal language and no preference for the term "Native."

Clearly, the question of what to call people whose ancestry lies in Pre-Columbian US territory is not a simple one and not one that can be answered with a single study on preferences. The heterogeneity of what people want to be called is an indicator of the complexity of identity. If it is impossible to select a single term, how can a single identity be possible? The rest of the chapters in this book highlight some aspects of the complex, multifaceted issue of identity of American Indian/Alaska Native, Native American, Indian, Native, Indigenous, and other people of the United States.

Note

1. It is worth noting that federally recognized tribal nations in the United States retain the ability to rely upon blood quantum, including setting the required blood quantum level itself, or lineal descent as a marker of tribal membership. Markers of membership vary among state recognized tribes. This will be discussed further in chapter 4. For more on blood quantum and its consequences for twenty-first-century American Indian identity, see Schmidt (2011).

CHAPTER THREE

~

"They're Not On and Off Switches"

Culture, History, and Heritage

According to Lakota scholar Hilary Weaver (2001), "Generally, identification is based on recognition of a common origin or shared characteristics with another person, group, or ideal leading to solidarity and allegiance. Beyond this, the discursive approach sees identification as an ongoing process that is never complete" (242). A Navajo *Native 24/7* participant echoed this sentiment when she stated, "Being *Diné*, what it means to me, it's the whole foundation of my culture. My clan systems, all my four clans, tells me where I'm from, tells me the people I come from, the characteristics in me."[1] A participant from the Southern Plains explained that he views himself as being both similar and simultaneously different from those around him:

> I come from a people who . . . have a different outlook on the world, and we understand the world differently, and we have a different language . . . culture . . . songs and ways that are kind of separate from mainstream America, but are similar to other American Indians. But, you know, we identify with American Indian people and yet we still take it a step forward, and we have even more of a specific identity, and knowing our songs or being aware of our languages that we speak in our religion, our dances and ceremonies, and then some of the values that we have that we were taught, carrying those and being aware of them.[2]

Native 24/7 participants identified a wide variety of influences on their understandings of both themselves and their communities when asked the open-ended question of what they believed were the major influences in their lives in terms of creating their Native identity. Participants explained that their identities were formed through a group of influencing factors that were both interpersonal and from their environments. Their answers fell into many categories, including primarily parents, grandparents, family in general, elders in the community, overall community, society at large outside of their communities, history, oral tradition and other traditional teachings or stories, government and policies, land and the greater natural environment, and teachers and formal schooling. Participants were asked specifically and separately about religion and spirituality as influences on their identity and discussed them extensively; these views are presented in chapter 5.

The most commonly mentioned influence named by participants in response to the open-ended question was family in general, with 35 percent of participants naming it. Many participants also named specific family members, including most notably parents (33%) and grandparents (29%). The next most commonly mentioned influence was history at 15 percent, followed by oral tradition or other traditional teachings at 9 percent. The dramatic difference in the number of people mentioning factors in the other categories of influences showcases the importance of family in defining identity. Therefore, family is discussed in detail in chapter 4. The current chapter focuses on personal and collective histories and heritage and their influence on culture and Native ways of life as important for reflecting on their everyday practices and for understanding themselves in the greater context of their communities. These types of influences were divided into history, oral tradition, government or policy, school or teachers for analysis by demographic factors (see figure 3.1 and table 3.1). Approximately 9 percent of participants talked about something entirely different as an influence, though nearly always tied to culture or way of life.

When examining differences in these influences by demographic factors, some trends emerged. The most consistent trend seen was that individuals who grew up in areas not on reservations or tribal trust land were more likely to talk about all of these factors. Individuals from reservation or tribal trust land communities were more likely to talk about some of the influences discussed in other chapters (e.g., family, spirituality). This may reflect a desire or need to learn about or further understand things like history and government when raised outside of a Native community. It may also reflect less importance placed on these topics among people who were raised in largely Native communities, with a greater importance placed on family and other influences. It is also possible that these participants did not want to talk about these topics with the interviewers for the project for whatever reason.

Because the number of individuals mentioning any of these factors when broken down by demographic factors is fairly low, it is difficult to interpret

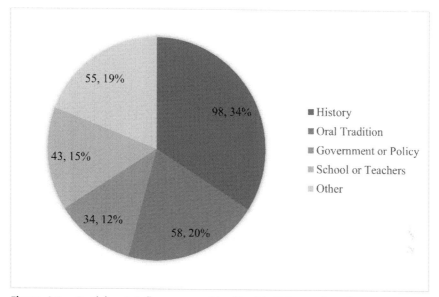

55, 19%

98, 34%

43, 15%

34, 12%

58, 20%

■ History

■ Oral Tradition

■ Government or Policy

■ School or Teachers

▨ Other

Figure 3.1. Participant Influences on Identity (N=288 mentions by participants). *Credit*: **Christine M. Daley, Charley Lewis, and Joseph Pacheco.**

many of the trends that arise. The trends could represent biases in the sample of people in this study rather than true trends; this is always true, but much more likely to be true with smaller numbers of individuals. This issue is particularly true when examining differences by culture area, though a few small trends are possible, including that individuals from the Great Lakes were more likely to discuss government or policy as an influence and individuals from the Southern Plains were more likely to label history and schools or teachers as influential.

Overall, oral tradition was discussed somewhat more by people enrolled in their tribe and somewhat less by people in the oldest age group (aged 50+), but these trends were not clear. It would appear that demographic factors did not impact in any significant way whether an individual discussed oral tradition as an influence on his or her identity.

The only trend that emerged by gender was that men may be more likely to talk about government or policy than women. In terms of age group, younger people (aged 18–29) tended to be more likely to talk about school or teachers influencing them. This is not surprising given that many of them were still in school or were recent graduates. They were less likely to talk about history or government and policy. This trend may reflect a disinterest in these topics, as is common among many young people. The oldest

Table 3.1. Participant Influences on Identity by Demographic Characteristics

Demographic Characteristic	History N (%)	Oral Tradition N (%)	Government or Policy N (%)	School or Teachers N (%)	Other N (%)
Gender (N=634)					
Male	39 (40%)	22 (38%)	19 (56%)	18 (42%)	21 (38%)
Female	59 (60%)	36 (62%)	15 (44%)	25 (58%)	34 (62%)
Age (N=634)					
18-29	22 (22%)	20 (34%)	7 (21%)	17 (40%)	15 (27%)
30-49	41 (42%)	24 (41%)	15 (44%)	18 (42%)	22 (40%)
50+	35 (36%)	14 (24%)	12 (35%)	8 (19%)	18 (33%)
Marital Status (N=603)					
Married/In a Relationship	55 (59%)	36 (64%)	21 (64%)	20 (49%)	31 (57%)
Never Married/ Divorced/ Separated/ Widowed	39 (41%)	20 (36%)	12 (36%)	21 (51%)	23 (43%)
Children (N=619)					
Yes	67 (70%)	39 (67%)	24 (71%)	17 (44%)	37 (67%)
No	29 (30%)	19 (33%)	10 (29%)	22 (56%)	18 (33%)
Education Level (N=621)					
GED or High School	16 (16%)	14 (25%)	6 (18%)	6 (15%)	16 (29%)
Post-High School Training or 2-year College Degree	38 (39%)	24 (42%)	8 (24%)	10 (24%)	20 (36%)
4-year College Degree or Higher	43 (44%)	19 (33%)	20 (59%)	25 (61%)	19 (35%)
Employment Status (N=615)					
Currently Employed	75 (79%)	41 (73%)	28 (82%)	34 (81%)	36 (65%)
Not Currently Employed	20 (21%)	15 (27%)	6 (18%)	8 (19%)	19 (35%)
American Indian Alone or Mixed Race (N=634)					
American Indian	68 (69%)	43 (74%)	26 (76%)	30 (70%)	45 (82%)
American Indian in Combination with Another Race/Ethnicity	30 (31%)	15 (26%)	8 (24%)	13 (30%)	10 (18%)

Demographic Characteristic	History N (%)	Oral Tradition N (%)	Government or Policy N (%)	School or Teachers N (%)	Other N (%)
Enrollment Status (N=618)					
Enrolled	79 (82%)	50 (86%)	25 (78%)	36 (84%)	43 (78%)
Not Enrolled	17 (18%)	8 (14%)	7 (22%)	7 (16%)	12 (22%)
Area Where Raised (N=623)					
Reservation or Tribal Trust Land	44 (45%)	26 (45%)	16 (47%)	18 (43%)	34 (62%)
Off-Reservation	53 (55%)	32 (55%)	18 (53%)	24 (57%)	21 (38%)
Culture Area (N=634)					
California	7 (7%)	6 (10%)	1 (3%)	4 (9%)	6 (11%)
Great Basin & Plateau	13 (13%)	4 (7%)	5 (15%)	3 (7%)	0 (0%)
Great Lakes	17 (17%)	11 (19%)	8 (24%)	7 (16%)	6 (11%)
Northeast & Southeast	17 (17%)	6 (10%)	11 (32%)	4 (9%)	3 (5%)
Northern Plains	7 (7%)	10 (17%)	1 (3%)	3 (7%)	15 (27%)
Northwest Coast, Arctic, Subarctic	7 (7%)	4 (7%)	2 (6%)	5 (12%)	2 (4%)
Southern Plains	25 (26%)	11 (19%)	6 (18%)	14 (33%)	4 (7%)
Southwest	5 (5%)	6 (10%)	0 (0%)	3 (7%)	19 (35%)

NOTE: Total N for each demographic variable are different based on whether or not an individual answered the demographic question. Percentages are presented as column percentages. Percentages may not total 100 due to rounding. The numbers in all columns represent the number of mentions by participants; participants could name multiple factors.

Credit: Christine M. Daley, Charley Lewis, and Joseph Pacheco

age group (aged 50+) was exactly the opposite, being more likely to talk about history, government, and policy and less likely to talk about school or teachers. This trend likely reflects changing views of the importance of these influences as people age.

Participants with children were less likely to talk about the influence of schools or teachers, as were people who were married or in a relationship. It is possible that these are the same people. Reasons for this are unclear, but may be related to the age of these individuals. They were more likely to be older, thus, their discussion of influencers may have been more driven by age than whether or not they interacted with a child's teacher or school system.

Education level appeared to have some influence on a participant's discussion of these topics. Individuals with the highest level of formal education (four-year college degree or higher) were more likely to talk about history, government or policy, and school or teachers as having an influence on their identities. Individuals with the lowest level of formal education (GED or high school) were less likely to discuss these topics. This trend is likely due to these factors being discussed in formal education and, of course, school or teachers, being a part of formal education. Employment status showed similar results, with individuals who were employed being more likely to talk about history, government or policy, and school or teachers as influencing their identity than those who were unemployed. These two factors, formal education and employment, are likely correlated.

Participants who claimed only Native ancestry as opposed to Native ancestry in combination with another race or ethnicity were less likely to talk about history and school or teachers, but no less likely to talk about government or policy. Participants who were enrolled in their tribe were somewhat more likely to talk about school or teachers, but no more likely to talk about history or government and policy.

Though all of these topics were not mentioned by a majority or even a large minority of participants, they appear to be important to those who discussed them. When the text of the interviews is examined more closely, the importance comes through in clearer ways, particularly the "other" category, which seemed to tie to different aspects of culture and way of life. These words exemplify participants' answers to the questions on the accompanying survey for the study focused on participation in cultural activities and keeping to a Native way of life. As discussed in chapter 1, participants placed a high value on this Native way of life, as well as on participation in activities of their own tribe and, to a lesser extent, those of other tribes. There was also interest in maintaining a Native community, with the majority of participants saying that many or most of their friends were from their tribe or another. These ideas, captured clearly by the survey data, were further explained in the interviews.

Culture and Way of Life

Though some scholars debate culture as a potential category for analysis because it is so abstract (Mitchell 1995; De Castro 2015; Graeber 2015; Kohn 2015), ideas of culture and cultural connections between individuals and communities were an important factor for *Native 24/7* participants in defining their Indigenous identities. As is often the case, the words of people outside of academe do not reflect currently scholarly debates, which often have little to no meaning to the average person. For the majority of *Native 24/7* participants, being a part of a Native culture, whether it was a tribal specific culture or more of a pan-Indian culture, adopting that culture as a way of life, and participating in that culture were exceptionally important, as was the history and heritage tied to that culture. Many *Native 24/7* participants stated that being Native was a way of life. "Being Native, what does it mean? Life."[3] was the statement made by one participant. According to a Creek participant, being Native *is* his everyday life. He explained:

Well, it's part of your everyday. It's when you wake up, it's when you go to sleep. You know, it's not an on and off switch. You don't stop being Creek or being Indian. . . . It's how you treat people. One of the things that's been instilled in me, my life, for a very long time has been to be Creek, to be Indian, is to be humble and love your neighbor. And that's something I try to carry with me throughout my days. So, that's what I try to live by, and then as far as other things that fall into that, knowing your history, knowing these traditions. I went to my ceremonial grounds this past weekend, danced, and played stickball. . . . It was a good time, but it was for all. You know, we do that stuff for the well-being of our entire tribe and to the extent of the well-being of all Indian people.[4]

Another participant stated that being Native gave her, "a way of life that covers the four aspects of human nature – the physical, the mental, the spiritual, and emotional . . . looking at it from that world view of a circle."[5] This quote reflects some participants' views that a holistic approach to life is the proper way to live as a Native person.

Many participants explained that it was not enough to believe oneself to be Native, but living as a member and engaging with the cultural and social traditions of one's community were of principle importance to being a member of these communities. One participant stated, "It means practicing the culture, maintaining those cultural values and practicing those traditions."[6] While another *Native 24/7* participant explained:

Being American Indian, to me, means participating in your tribal culture, whether participating in pow wows, whether that's participating in ceremony, or going to gather medicinal plants, go gather your wild game, all of those things mean that you are American Indian . . . even in the urban settings, being in touch with, you know, a lot of our urban cities have American Indian centers, and finding ways to participate and be involved. Knowing your culture, knowing your heritage. If you are affiliated with a federally recognized tribe, that would mean knowing your treaties, knowing your homelands, where your people lived, what they subsisted off of. All of those things are really important and contribute to being American Indian.[7]

A tribal elder said that to him, being Native, "means embracing my culture, and having it make me a better person. To participate in all the cultural activities. It is important for the children and grandchildren to see us in that light. That way they can identify with who they are based on how they see their grandparents, parents, siblings participate in the culture also."[8] Another participant stated being Native, "It's a way of life and a belief system. I think it's the way . . . you carry yourself and interact with the world around you, the things that you value, the things you participate in, and the way you communicate with the world."[9]

The consensus among participants who talked about this topic seemed to be that it is not the right thing to simply claim an Indigenous identity; rather, identity was seen as a lived experience in combination with a community of Native people around you. This may suggest that community participation gives rise to certain feelings of Indigeneity and connects a person to his or her culture and other members of it. This reflects findings in other contexts that suggest the embodied and emplaced experiences of individuals elicit certain understandings of self in a broader community (Pink 2005; Pink 2011).

Native 24/7 participants frequently felt that someone needed to have knowledge about Native and tribal ways of life to claim Native identity. A young Navajo participant explained that to her, "being Dine' means . . . understanding your culture, your history, your language, your traditions. And not just understanding, but also . . . teaching part of it. You can't just say that you like peanut butter and jelly, but then you never tried it or anything like that. So, you can't say that I'm Navajo, but then not do anything at all . . . yeah, you can be Navajo, but I think that it's important that you know all the aspects in being Navajo or *Diné*."[10]

A participant from the Northern Plains commented that:

American Indian . . . it is like a broad spectrum. To me, it is not like it was before, you know? Sometimes I feel like people have lost their ways or something like that. So, how can they consider themselves American Indian or Native American . . . if they don't know where they came from; how can they go into the future and call themselves that? That is kind of a hard question to ask, you know? But to me, myself, American Indian, it's not growing up on a reservation, it's learning your ways and living them day by day and remembering everything that was taught to you and then passing them on to your kids.[11]

This idea that Native people who do not know their cultures and ways are somehow lost was echoed by one participant who said the following:

Being an Indian is not like a tradition, it is just our way of life. Our language, too, which is trying to come back on the rez. . . . But, as far as it means living the old ways, the way things were the old way, the traditional way, that is what being Indian means to me, really. . . . But some people on the rez don't know about that. There are . . . people that come to our ceremonies and stuff like that and try to learn about our living and traditional ways. But we still have a lot of young people who don't know who they are. They are practicing other backgrounds . . . they are going around like hoodlums . . . they are dressing like them, talking like them, and having slang like them. So, you know, it is really learning about who we are, who we really are, and then that way they do not have to pretend to be someone else who they are not, taking on someone else's identity. To me they are lost.[12]

An Ojibwa elder explained that even though he was forced to go to boarding school, he did not lose his way and was still proud of being Native, and that pride is what kept him from going down the wrong path in life. He explained:

I grew up in, I went to boarding schools. When I was seven years old, there were a lot of things that went on in that time, and then after I got out of there, there were a lot of things that happened then too. . . . One time, these brothers and priests in boarding school, they asked me a question, 'What do you think of this place?' And I said, 'I don't know.' And I still don't know. . . . Being Native American is something you should be proud of, I always believed, you know. I learned to become very proud . . . of my heritage because of that. Because things were trying to be pushed into my head. . . . But I have to say being proud of who you are, practicing your culture . . . that's really important. That's something I do; my whole family does. We practice the traditional way; the Ojibwa way. . . . I think you have to really understand who you are. If you don't, I think you're going to be totally lost, and you're going to be going on the wrong road, the wrong path.[13]

A Lakota participant from Standing Rock noted that culture was pretty much all they had on his reservation. He stated, "We don't have much back home (Standing Rock). We don't have rich land. We don't have money coming in like other tribes. We grew up having ourselves, our ceremonies, our pow wows. That's what I hold dear to my heart. That's what that means to me."[14]

Another participant echoed his sentiment and explained it further with examples of the problems on her reservation, "I was born and raised on a reservation, seeing what everyone was going through . . . people coming in . . . drunks, diabetics, alcoholics, and heroin addicts. . . . I grew up wanting to give back to my community. . . . I was always taught to respect the older generation, and we have a lot of boys that are traditional. . . . Being Native American means to me taking pride in our culture and our land and our natural resources."[15]

History and Heritage
In addition to culture and a Native way of life being identified as key to many participants' views of what it means to be Native, history and heritage played into many participants' views as well. A young Navajo participant explained, "It gives me a self-identity. I think the fact that we know we have history here on the land dating many years back and how our ancestors suffered for us to be here, and when you think . . . how the Navajo people have emerged through the Four Worlds and . . . the Long Walk and how we've sacrificed a lot of things to create treaties for us to remain on our land, I think it gives me a self-identity and tells me who I am . . . my clan and how people around me are related to me. I think that gives me power and strength to face the challenges that we face today."[16]

One participant stated that being Native "means trying to learn the ways of our people that have come before us and continuing . . . our culture and practices . . . being respectful of myself and others, and where they are coming from . . . trying to be a role model . . . and showing our kids and future generations that there are possibilities, and that things don't always have to be a struggle. . . . In general, I think we all should be learning our heritage and continuing that through stories, practices, participating in dancing and singing, and all of those things."[17]

An O'odham participant stated that even though things have changed greatly for his people, there is still pride in their history. He explained, "We're called the Akimel O'odham; it means the 'River People.' . . . Well to me, it has a history. . . . Throughout the reservation (Arizona) there used to be a river, but it got dammed and now it's dried up. So, being called the River People, to me, holds a sense of history . . . something that can't be taken away from us because the river's still there even though it's not flowing."[18] Historic ties to the land were important to many participants and were often tied to their ancestors. This connection of the land to ancestors and family is discussed in chapter 4.

Other values connected to Native heritage were very important in many participants' views of what it means to be Native. "Holding my traditional values, holding what my ancestors taught me . . . to the highest level possible"[19] was what one individual stated was most important to her in defining what it meant to be Native. Another participant stated that a Native is "someone who holds values and traditions and culture and passes (them) down. Who started off a long time ago passing the traditions on orally from generation to generation, and someone who still practices their culture; who doesn't believe in one god, but many gods and incorporates different values and traditions and uses that through language and songs, and different non-

Christian things . . . using medicine and herbs and prayers."[20] An Ojibwe participant stated that being "Ojibwe means to me . . . being proud . . . of my people's ways and trying to carry them on the best that I can and learn my language . . . keep my language intact, and you know, do the best that I can every day."[21]

A Navajo participant explained that in order to be Navajo, one must try to follow traditional customs and values. He explained:

> Being Navajo, to me, means adhering, following a lot of traditional Navajo customs. It means recognizing who you are and knowing where you come from, and your history as well. It goes for practically every tribe. To me, being Navajo is something that I hold very dear to my heart . . . it's something that really defines me and who I am and how I interact with people. And so specifically being Navajo I try to adhere to as much of traditional values as I can. But at times it becomes difficult living in a White society.[22]

Finally, pride in one's Native history and heritage was integral to many participants' identities. A twenty-one-year-old Navajo/Lakota participant stated, "I'm a descendant of Wounded Knee and I am a descendant of the Long Walk. I have a great-grandpa who was one of the original 28 Code Talkers. I'm really proud of who I am and where I come from; what my people persevered for me to be here now and for me to hang onto our culture and hopefully learn it and teach it to the younger generation."[23]

A Kiowa elder noted that it was his feeling that "it's an honor; it's a great spiritual feeling to be Native American. My ancestors, my grandparents, were medicine people. . . . My tribe, which is the Kiowa of Oklahoma . . . could walk in their tracks to be able to pray with their pipes, their staffs, their warrior staffs, their tomahawks, their arrows, their horns, their medicine bags that I keep, the medicine bundles that I keep. It's a beautiful honor to walk in their tracks."[24]

"Being Native American means being part of a cultural background . . . having a lot of really great traditions within our family and to go back to the roots of the first people that were here on American soil. And it's actually something to be pretty proud of, and such a great group of people around you to support that whole culture and the ancestors that were here once upon a time ago."[25]

A participant from Acoma Pueblo noted that she was proud that the people of Acoma have continued to practice their ways for such a long time. She stated, "Being Native American means being proud of who I am. I'm proud of where I come from and what tribe I'm from (Acoma) 'cause we take our traditions seriously, and it has been continuous and we still practice it today. So, to me, it means everything that I am and everything that I teach my family starts from where I come from."[26]

Another participant noted that she was proud that she was passing her ways on to her children and that they were going to walk the Red Road. She said, "Being Native American, to me, means that I know my kids are going to grow up knowing the right way to walk the Red Road,[27] and to be proud of what they are. I'm proud of what I am; my heritage and everything else."[28]

Some *Native 24/7* participants, however, noted that being Native had drawbacks as well. One participant noted that to him "Indigenous kind of means being active within your culture. And attempting to live . . . as best you can given the current predicament . . . living in a very European-American society. So, sometimes I think being Indigenous or Native is trying to almost maintain that identity while these kinds of outside forces are maybe belittling or attacking our identity."[29]

Another participant stated that being Native comes with pros and cons. She explained that being Native "means a lot of different things. I guess on one level my ancestors are Native, which because of colonization and policies and practices related to colonization means I come from very resilient people with lots of strengths and a lot of healing to be done. It also means that in society, in general, there is a lot of racism and misconceptions, lack of information, health disparities, lots of work that needs to be done."[30]

One elder stated, "I'm very proud of my heritage, but I am also distressed over the fact that our government has all but eliminated the history of Native Americans and what they've done to them in the past. It has been taken out of the history books. We're not being honest with future generations."[31]

Drawbacks to Native Identity
Though it was not the norm, some participants talked about the problems with having and, more specifically, claiming a Native heritage. Conflict and difficulties with mainstream Americans and mainstream American culture were named as being an unfortunate part of Native identity. A Lakota elder stated,

Well, to me, as a Lakota . . . it means living your way of life. It's not just an enrollment card or your tribal connections, saying, 'Well, I am this or I am that,' it's really living it and it's a way of life that oftentimes conflicts with the dominant culture. It creates a lot of misunderstanding and a lack of knowledge and ignorance, especially in part of the dominant culture. As I would say they know more about us than we know about them. And we remain that sort of invisible race. But to be Indian to me is to understand the relationship to all things, that we are related to all things, everything is related, everything we do. It's about respect for all things, all colors, all races, different religious beliefs . . . it's just a beautiful way of life. It's a hard way of life to live in such a place like America because of the laws and just some of the things that clash with us and our culture.[32]

One participant equated being Native with being a wild animal. He stated, "Being Native American, to me, means that we are unlike any other race. Our people die off slowly because of the way we have to live. Our ways are going to disappear. We have to adapt like an animal in this world."[33] Another participant noted that Natives are unlike any other racial or ethnic minority group in the United States. He explained:

Being Native American . . . it means that I'm a minority. It means that I am economically disadvantaged; it means that in some cases if I play the game right, then maybe there are different opportunities available to me because of my economically disadvantaged situation. . . . It also means that, you know, I'm a part of a people that have once roamed this area I guess, free to do as they will, and so I mean it – I've got a sense of belonging in America, regardless of what anybody makes me feel or anything like that when I work . . . when I'm working or employed at a position outside my race. It's also difficult at times being Native American working with White people or Black people or Asians, just Americans in general. It's really different because we have a different value system.[34]

Embarrassment and concern were issues for some participants. One woman from the Great Lakes area stated, "I'm going to be honest. . . . I'm Native American [but] I almost feel like I'm being a fraud. I was raised White; I was raised White in a White neighborhood. My grandfather was ashamed of his heritage. He was in an Indian school and was taught to be ashamed, so we were raised White. It's only been within the past couple of years that I myself have begun to identify and seek out and learn more about it and incorporate some of the culture into the way that I live my life."[35]

Another participant, also from the Great Lakes, explained, "I'm 52 years of age and my grandmother raised me, so she used to take me to the UP (Upper Peninsula) and go to tribal events there . . . but yet at the same time as a child, I was told to say that I was White."[36]

Conclusion

Clearly, culture, history, and heritage are significant contributing factors to the identities of many *Native 24/7* participants. For most participants being a part of a Native culture, adopting that culture as a way of life, and participating in that culture were exceptionally important, as was knowing the history and heritage tied to that culture. "It's a lot about family, culture, and tradition,"[37] stated one participant. Another participant explained, "Being Native American, to me, means that you are putting pride with your culture above being . . . assimilated into today's society, learning your language and your culture and passing on, and educating others who don't know about you or your tribe."[38] Other *Native 24/7* participants took it further and stated that being Native was what life is all about. According to a Muscogee elder, "I was born and raised . . . Muscogee Creek . . . it's been all my life. . . . So I haven't really had time to think about it. I'm just Indian."[39] Another participant simply explained, "I've always been Native. . . . I woke up this way."[40] But what does that mean?

According to the Shawnee, Sac and Fox, Muscogee Creek and Seminole scholar Donald Fixico (1995), "To be an 'Indian' involves a spectrum of identities from a generic Indianness to tribal culture, social need, societal judgement, and psychological self-examination. Placed in historical perspective, the range of meanings for 'to be an Indian' has varied as each generation and each group's tribal existence is juxtaposed to or integrated into the American mainstream" (ix). The statements made by *Native 24/7* participants and the stories they shared echo this statement, including both the good and the bad. Participants also showcased the variety of identities meant by these generic statements of "being an Indian" by discussing history and culture specific to their tribes. As explained by Choctaw scholar Devon Mihesuah (1998), "Tribes are not alike. They have different languages, religions, histories, and methods of dealing with non-Indians. . . . The historical time period of the person's life must be taken into account. . . . Their physiologies, images among non-Indians, and individual and tribal socioeconomic situations are different, as are their world views. . . . Even within a group, the personal needs, physiology, and environmental influences of each individual is different" (198). It would appear that the uniqueness of each individual culture and each individual within that culture is what being Indian is.

Though ties to culture and heritage were only discussed by a minority of participants in the interviews, 96 percent of participants named personal maintenance of their tribe's Native identity, values, and practices as important in the accompanying surveys. Clearly, these things are more important than discussed in the interviews. It is likely that some of the other influences named by participants, particularly family influence and the influence of spirituality, are intricately entwined with culture and heritage. The next few chapters will explore these issues in depth.

Notes

1. 30-year-old female from a Southwestern reservation community.
2. 34-year-old male from a Southern Plains reservation community.
3. 50-year-old male from a Southern Plains rural community.
4. 32-year-old male from a Southern Plains urban community.
5. 54-year-old female from a Great Lakes urban community.
6. 33-year-old male participant from a Northwest Coast reservation community.
7. 25-year-old female from a Plateau reservation community.
8. 60-year-old male from a Great Lakes reservation community.
9. 32-year-old female from a Plateau urban community.
10. 24-year-old female from a Great Basin rural community.
11. 40-year-old male from a Northern Plains reservation community.
12. 45-year-old female from a Northern Plains rural community.
13. 64-year-old male from a Northern Plains reservation community.
14. 29-year-old male from a Northern Plains reservation community.
15. 30-year-old female from a California urban community.
16. 25-year-old male from a Southwestern reservation community.
17. 31-year-old female from a Plateau reservation community.
18. 21-year-old male from a Southwestern rural community.
19. 30-year-old female from a Great Basin reservation community.
20. 20-year-old female from a Southwestern reservation community.
21. 25-year-old male from a Great Lakes urban community.
22. 18-year-old male from a Southwestern urban community.
23. 21-year-old female from a Southwestern reservation community.
24. 58-year-old male from a Southern Plains rural community.
25. 21-year-old female from a Southern Plains community.
26. 36-year-old female from a Southwestern reservation community.
27. Although there are different interpretations, most often the Red Road refers to living life with a purpose and one focused on positive change.
28. 34-year-old female from a Southwestern urban community.
29. 33-year-old male from a Southern Plains rural community.
30. 30-year-old female from a Great Lakes urban community.
31. 74-year-old male from a Southern Plains rural community.
32. 67-year-old male from a Northern Plains urban community.
33. 22-year-old male from a Northern Plains rural community.
34. 31-year-old male from a Southern Plains urban community.
35. 40-year-old female from a Great Lakes urban community.
36. 52-year-old female from a Great Lakes rural community.
37. 19-year-old female from a Great Lakes urban community.
38. 21-year-old female from a California reservation community.
39. 63-year-old male from a Southern Plains rural community.
40. 33-year-old female from a Great Lakes urban community.

CHAPTER FOUR

~

"Natives, We're Good Relatives"

Family, Community, and Relationships

An Anishinaabe Creation Story

When the Earth was young, it had a family. The Moon is called Grand-mother, and the Sun is called Grandfather. This family is the basis of all creation in the universe. This family was created by *Gitchi Manitou*, the Cre-ator. Earth is said to be a woman. She preceded man and her name is Mother Earth because all living things live from her gifts. Water is her life blood. It flows through her, nourishes her, and purifies her.

Mother Earth was given Four Sacred Directions—North, South, East, and West. Each direction contributes a vital part of her wholeness. Each direction and all things on Mother Earth have physical powers and spiritual powers.

When she was young, Mother Earth was filled with beauty. The Creator sent his singers in the form of birds to carry the seeds of life to all of the Four Sacred Directions. Life was spread across the land. The Creator placed the swimming creatures in the water. He placed the crawling things and the four-legged animals on the land. He gave life to all the plants and insects of the world. All parts of life lived in harmony with each other on Mother Earth.

Gitchi Manitou took the four parts of Mother Earth and blew them into a sacred *megis* shell. From the union of the Four Sacred Elements and his breath, man was created. It is said that *Gitchi Manitou* then lowered man to the Earth. Thus, man was the last form of life to be placed on Earth. From this Original Man came the *Anishinaabe* people. This man was created in the image of *Gitchi Manitou*. Man was part of Mother Earth. He lived in brotherhood with all life that surrounded him (Parks Canada 2018).

Although just one example, the above narrative illustrates an important theme that ran throughout the entirety of conversations with participants in *Native 24/7*. Regardless of the question asked, participants routinely described the importance of interpersonal relationships, particularly with family members, in realizing, understanding, and practicing their identities. This apparent connection is not a new approach; there is an intense focus on interpersonal relationships by many scholars of identity across the social sciences (Ehala 2018; Polletta and Jasper 2001; Jasper 1997; Erikson 1966). *Native 24/7* participants also described further influences that went beyond friends and family to include ancestral relationships and, in some cases, relationships with place. This focus reflects critiques by Indigenous scholars that suggest scholarly frameworks for understanding identity and belonging may be too narrow or ill-equipped to understand Indigenous ideas of these concepts (Alfred and Corntassel 2005; Weaver 2001).

For many Native peoples, it is not enough to understand oneself in the context of blood relatives, but rather it is important to understand the complex network of relationships and obligations that are an integral part of being a member of a community. This perception revealed itself repeatedly throughout conversations with *Native 24/7* participants. As described in previous chapters, when asked about influences on their identities, *Native 24/7* participants had many answers, including the traditions, customs, languages of their tribes, as well as the tribes of others, interactions with other Native peoples, interactions and dealings with non-Native peoples, their educational experiences, and American society as a whole. However, relationships with family and community members, including ancestral connections, were seen as centrally important to understanding oneself as a Native person. In some cases, participants extended these relationships beyond interpersonal connections to include an understanding of oneself in relationship to the land or other parts of the environment.

Participant explanations of family, community, and environmental influences on identity were categorized into parents, grandparents, other family members or family in general, elders outside their family, their home community, US society as a whole, and references to land or other aspects of the natural environment to better understand the importance of these influences on different types of people. Thirty-three percent of participants named their parents as influential in terms of their Native identity and 29 percent named their grandparents. An additional 35 percent of participants named a different family member or family in general as influential. All other influences in this area were discussed by far fewer participants, with 12 percent of participants mentioning their community, 8 percent mentioning the natural environment, 6 percent mentioning society at large, and 5 percent mentioning elders.

Family and Culture

The overwhelming majority of participants, across all demographic factors, stated that their families were the first and most influential factor in their identities, though female participants were somewhat more likely to talk about family than their male counterparts. There were small variations in which family member(s) were most important, with a particular emphasis placed on older generations (parents and grandparents) among participants in the youngest age category (age 18–29). Participants with mixed ancestry were more likely to focus on non-parent or grandparent relatives, instead talking about family in a general sense or other family members; they also tended to focus on the greater Native community and influences of society at large more than participants who claimed only Native ancestry (see figure 4.1 and table 4.1).

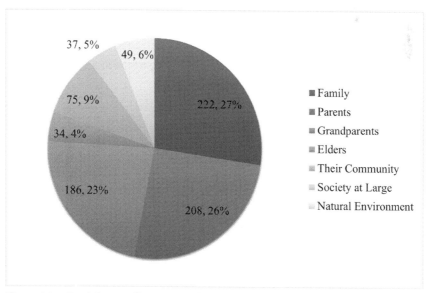

Figure 4.1. Participant Influences on Identity: Family & Community (N=811 mentions by participants). *Credit:* **Christine M. Daley, Charley Lewis, and Joseph Pacheco.**

Table 4.1. Participant Influences on Identity: Family & Community by Demographic Characteristics

Demographic Characteristic	Family N (%)	Parents N (%)	Grandparents N (%)	Elders N (%)	Their Community N (%)	Society at Large N (%)	Natural Environment N (%)
Gender (N=634)							
Male	78 (35%)	77 (37%)	69 (37%)	13 (38%)	30 (40%)	21 (43%)	19 (51%)
Female	144 (65%)	131 (63%)	117 (63%)	21 (62%)	45 (60%)	28 (57%)	18 (49%)
Age (N=634)							
18-29	78 (35%)	70 (34%)	68 (37%)	9 (26%)	25 (33%)	18 (37%)	11 (30%)
30-49	86 (39%)	76 (37%)	63 (34%)	17 (50%)	34 (45%)	17 (35%)	18 (49%)
50+	58 (26%)	62 (33%)	55 (30%)	8 (24%)	16 (21%)	14 (29%)	8 (22%)
Marital Status (N=603)							
Married/In a Relationship	127 (59%)	107 (53%)	94 (53%)	20 (59%)	41 (58%)	27 (59%)	22 (61%)
Never Married/Divorced/Separated/Widowed	88 (41%)	95 (47%)	83 (47%)	14 (41%)	30 (42%)	19 (41%)	14 (39%)
Children (N=619)							
Yes	147 (67%)	135 (66%)	130 (71%)	26 (76%)	49 (67%)	28 (61%)	21 (58%)
No	72 (33%)	70 (34%)	54 (29%)	8 (24%)	24 (33%)	18 (39%)	15 (42%)
Education Level (N=621)							
GED or High School	49 (22%)	51 (25%)	54 (29%)	7 (21%)	14 (19%)	15 (32%)	6 (17%)
Post-High School Training or 2-year College Degree	91 (42%)	97 (48%)	76 (41%)	16 (47%)	30 (41%)	18 (38%)	12 (33%)
4-year College Degree or Higher	79 (36%)	56 (27%)	54 (29%)	11 (32%)	29 (40%)	14 (30%)	18 (50%)
Employment Status (N=615)							
Currently Employed	156 (72%)	138 (68%)	121 (67%)	27 (82%)	52 (72%)	33 (70%)	28 (78%)
Not Currently Employed	60 (28%)	66 (32%)	59 (33%)	6 (18%)	20 (28%)	14 (30%)	8 (22%)

American Indian Alone or Mixed Race (N=634)

American Indian	163 (73%)	159 (76%)	146 (78%)	27 (79%)	53 (71%)	32 (65%)	25 (68%)
American Indian in Combination with Another Race/Ethnicity	59 (27%)	49 (24%)	40 (22%)	7 (21%)	22 (29%)	17 (35%)	12 (32%)
Enrollment Status (N=618)							
Enrolled	177 (81%)	169 (84%)	149 (83%)	24 (73%)	20 (27%)	10 (21%)	32 (86%)
Not Enrolled	41 (19%)	32 (16%)	31 (17%)	9 (27%)	54 (73%)	37 (79%)	5 (14%)
Area Where Raised (N=623)							
Reservation or Tribal Trust Land	112 (51%)	111 (54%)	96 (52%)	17 (50%)	39 (53%)	21 (45%)	23 (64%)
Off-Reservation	107 (49%)	95 (46%)	89 (48%)	17 (50%)	34 (47%)	26 (55%)	13 (36%)
Culture Area (N=634)							
California	17 (8%)	22 (11%)	19 (10%)	4 (12%)	3 (4%)	3 (6%)	3 (8%)
Great Basin & Plateau	19 (9%)	22 (11%)	23 (12%)	5 (15%)	10 (13%)	9 (18%)	4 (11%)
Great Lakes	41 (18%)	34 (16%)	34 (18%)	6 (18%)	18 (24%)	18 (37%)	5 (14%)
Northeast & Southeast	28 (13%)	19 (9%)	6 (3%)	3 (9%)	8 (11%)	8 (16%)	7 (19%)
Northern Plains	32 (14%)	34 (16%)	31 (17%)	4 (12%)	8 (11%)	2 (4%)	2 (5%)
Northwest Coast, Arctic, Subarctic	15 (7%)	14 (7%)	12 (6%)	2 (6%)	5 (7%)	7 (14%)	4 (11%)
Southern Plains	45 (20%)	39 (19%)	34 (18%)	4 (12%)	20 (27%)	2 (4%)	8 (22%)
Southwest	25 (11%)	24 (12%)	27 (15%)	6 (18%)	3 (4%)	0 (0%)	4 (11%)

NOTE: Total N for each demographic variable are different based on whether or not an individual answered the demographic question. Percentages are presented as column percentages. Percentages may not total to 100 due to rounding. The numbers in all columns represent the number of mentions by participants; participants could name multiple factors.

Credit: Christine M. Daley, Charley Lewis, and Joseph Pacheco

One participant simply stated, "If you're a true Native, you know Native ways . . . family is central."[1] When asked about who or what most influenced her identity, one participant noted:

> First and foremost, my family. My mom and dad come from two different nations. They grounded me with a sense of identity as a Native person. . . . I've also married outside to another tribe. I have adopted relatives in other tribes, and so I think we really as Native people, we all possess a commonality. Like in the Lakota way, they say *mitakye oyasin*, which is a philosophy that you're acknowledging your relationship with all of creation. And I think truly in every Native community or nation, that's what we are. We're good relatives.[2]

Family is a cultural universal, meaning all peoples, communities, and cultures have "family," but what constitutes "family" can vary greatly. As noted by the cultural anthropologist Conrad Phillip Kottak (2016), "The term *family* . . . is basic, familiar . . . and difficult to define in a way that applies to all cultures" (132). Among Westerners, it is common to define family as parents and their young unmarried children residing in the same household, often referred to as a nuclear family. This definition is maintained institutionally, as well as socially, through mechanisms such as the United States Census definition of family as "a group of two people or more [one of whom is the householder] related by birth, marriage, or adoption and residing together" (United States Census Bureau 2020).

Participants' families featured prominently in their discussions of influences on their lives and identities. Unsurprisingly, given their cultural and historical importance for many Native communities (Liddell et al. 2021), participants' mothers were frequently identified as important figures in their lives. According to one participant,

> I attribute a lot to my mom, instilling simple Native pride in me. Being so far away from a reservation or any Native community really, I'd have to attribute a lot to her, not only instilling pride, but also teaching me along the way, as I was growing up, how our reservation is, teaching me I was part of the Iroquois Nation, learning from the Iroquois tribes of what their different cultural ways were, what their dances are, and their relationship with lacrosse and to the Higher Being, and then just kind of visiting different tribal leaders as they came through and being able to chat with them. Without my mom, it would be really hard to stay connected to being a Native person and holding cultural ties not only to my reservation, but to cultural knowledge.[3]

Another participant explained that his mother taught him everything. He noted that she, "taught me every aspect of life . . . from tying my shoes to using my mind. . . . She taught me to be the person I am. . . . I feel like my mother did the impossible, raised a man, or a house full of men."[4]

Fathers were important figures for many *Native 24/7* participants as well. One participant emphasized that it was his father who influenced him. He simply stated, "My father . . . he taught me the ways of the Red Road and . . . to respect Mother Earth and not to always go with what I think of as American Indian, you know?"[5]

The important role played by parents within the family was likewise recognized by individuals who were themselves parents. One participant stated that it was having children that most influenced her identity. She said, "I feel, truly feel, that . . . I didn't know who I was, what my purpose was, until I became a mom. And once I became a mom, my culture and heritage, my religious beliefs, everything became more focused, more centered, more important in my life because of who I wanted my children to be."[6] It should be noted, however, that individuals with children were no more likely to talk about family than those without children. It was instead the way the family members influenced them that was different, but not the importance of family connections.

Many non-Western and Indigenous peoples around the world define family differently than many individuals in mainstream American society do. Typically, these definitions are more encompassing and not as restrictive (Light and Martin 1986; Tam, Findlay, and Kohen 2017). It is common for non-Westerners and Indigenous peoples to include what Westerners call grandparents, aunts, uncles, and cousins as primary family as well, rather than being relegated to a Western sense of the nuclear family (Tam et al. 2017). Indigenous conceptions of both fatherhood and motherhood are understood more broadly to include male and female relatives like aunts and uncles, as well as others in a family's social network (Hall et al. 2020; Liddell et al. 2021). Aunts and uncles on one side of the family may also be defined differently than aunts and uncles on the other side of the family. For example, among matrilineal peoples, kinship is passed down first and foremost through the mother's line. In this case, the mother's brother (whom we call uncle in the United States) is usually higher in status and has more of an obligation to his nephews and nieces than the father's brother (also called uncle in the United States). As one participant explained, his paternal uncle, a totem pole carver, influenced him the most. He explained, "I would have to say that the person who has influenced me the most was my Uncle Glen. . . . We sat there and watched him carve. . . . I was probably about nine years old when I realized that I was Haida, and finding out what was with that, being

Haida, and the journey that came with being Haida. We carved large totem poles and the stories of us that are on these poles. . . . Our people are great artists. That's why I identify with that."[7]

Grandparents were also cited as a significant influence on identity by *Native 24/7* participants. Those who are familiar with Native family structure are aware that grandparents are integral caregivers to their grandchildren, and are often responsible for raising their grandchildren, especially in situations where the parents are absent or unable to do so (Cross, Day, and Byers 2010; Mutchler, Baker, and Lee 2007). One participant noted that her grandparents had a significant effect on her Native identity by teaching her to be proud that she was different than those around her. She explained:

They always taught me, you know, obviously our traditional values . . . why we are different from other people. I remember coming home crying because we didn't live on the reservation when I first started school and I was like I don't understand why people don't like me and she (my grandmother) said they don't like you for who you are and it took me a long time to figure it out . . . getting beat up at school or getting picked on at school because of my skin color or because I went to school with two little Indian braids. My grandparents always told me you're Indian, you're Native American, that's who you're always going to be . . . and be who I am . . . that's who we are as Native people.[8]

Another participant said, "My grandma used to say if you walk that Red Road, then you shouldn't have any problem being who you are and knowing who you are. She told us to carry ourselves in a respectful manner because not only are we out there representing our tribe, but we're representing them as well—representing our parents and grandparents."[9] One participant from the Northern Plains saw the importance of her grandparents' knowledge related to the history of cultural and language loss. She explained:

My whole family . . . from grandparents on down. Grandparents mainly had humble ways; they had the original way 'cause they were taught by their grandparents. Their moms and dads, they're the ones that lived in the old way. So, the way that we are now, it's different, it's like our parents, they know some of the ways, but they got caught up in Western society . . . that's why a lot of people now are lost. They don't have language, they don't know anything about their culture or anything besides, you know, going to a pow wow or somewhere like that. But they don't really know the meaning behind what they're doing because they weren't taught that way. . . . My whole family was involved in everything, it wasn't just my grandparents, it was my grandparents' brothers and sisters, they all had a part in our teaching and what we doing when we grew up.[10]

Grandparents, specifically, were also often cited by participants as being the source of traditions connected to spirituality and identity, reflecting findings from previous research (Robbins et al. 2005). Participants often described how grandparents were instrumental in exposing them to a variety of spiritual practices and encouraging them to practice them for themselves as a marker of their identity as Native peoples. This most often included Native spiritual traditions and the Native American Church, but also included various Christian denominations as well. One participant described how his grandfather influenced him through his practice of spiritual traditions. He said that his grandfather "used to wake up every morning and smudge the house and just play the drum and listen to the flute during the afternoon. So, it kind of encouraged me. He had me dance and play the drum when I was in elementary school. . . . He influenced me a lot on my religion and my beliefs."[11]

A Navajo participant explained that his grandfather's spiritual role in their community was particularly influential. He explained, "My grandpa was a shaman . . . he was one of those crystal gazers, and also Native American Church. . . . He did the Navajo traditional ceremonies . . . he had held all those beliefs. . . . It was a philosophy of life and teachings, teachings of how to live your life, and that's why I've always known where I am going, where I come from, and where I'll be going."[12] Another *Native 24/7* participant explained, "My maternal grandpa . . . he didn't go to school, but he was very wise and smart, and I learned a lot from him, and I think that's a lot of where I come from as a person and everything I know about traditional ways or even my religion. Going to Native American Church, that's where I developed who I am and where I am supposed to be in life."[13]

Other participants described how these connections with their grandparents through spirituality helped them to reflect on their community's history as well. One Dakota participant explained, "When I was growing up, my grandfather taught me a lot about our ways, so I'm very involved in making sure I maintain a Native identity. . . . That's how I was raised since I was a little boy. . . . They taught me about the spiritual path that every Native American should at least follow in their lives if they grew up around it. . . . And another event that put me on a track to really help me understand why I'm on a spiritual path with my family is the Dakota 38 hangings,[14] which is the biggest mass hanging in US history. Thirty-eight Dakota men were hung and of the 38, pretty much all of them . . . were medicine men."[15]

Community Relations

In Native America, clans, bands, moieties, and other groupings also come into play representing broader, community-level relationships for many Native peoples. For example, among the Diné (Navajo), a matrilineal society, clans are of utmost importance. "All Navajos belong to a matrilineal clan composed of large groups of relatives identified with a common female ancestor. . . . A Navajo is Born To the mother's clan and Born For the father's clan" (Parezo 1996, 7). This was supported by a Navajo participant who stated:

> So . . . being Navajo, when we do our introductions, we always introduce who our clans are. Because . . . our introduction isn't about who we are as an individual, about what we've done, about how much money we make, or where we work, or where we went to school. It gives you, like, a story of our history, and it talks about your clans and who you're related to, and then it talks about . . . your mother's side, cause they're matrilineal, a matrilineal society. Then our father's origins, and also . . . who our ancestors are and how we are all related, and that's just kind of our way we introduce ourselves. So, you don't start with yourself because you are not here because of you, you're here because of your ancestors, and because of everyone else.[16]

Broader connections like this example were often mentioned by our participants in addition to their immediate families. For instance, among the Lakota, *tiyospaye*, or extended family, are significant and can include *hunka*, or adopted kin (White Hat and Cunnigham 2012). This reflects that, for many Indigenous communities, the concept of family extends beyond blood relations to include a wide variety of other members of their community, as well as relationships to place and other-than-human beings. For *Native 24/7* participants, as described previously, family included mothers, fathers, siblings, grandparents, aunts, uncles, cousins, spouses, children, spouses' families, and so on. Family also included greater social connections, like clans, communities, and tribes. As noted previously, 12 percent of participants mentioned their Native community as influential and an additional 5 percent named elders from their community specifically. Among these individuals, working parents in the 30- to 49-year age group mentioned the greater Native community more than others, potentially again reflecting their views as parents that their children need to learn about Native identity, in this case, from everyone around them. Younger people (aged 18–29) were more likely to speak specifically about elders.

"It's about being a part of your community . . . not just of course having blood, but being a part of your community; being active, knowing some of your language, if not speaking it fluently, and learning your traditional values and ways of doing things,"[17] commented one participant. Another participant stated that strong family ties and a connection to his community were important to him. He explained, "To me, being Native is about your values, the way you were growing up, the way you were raised, and how you present yourself in public . . . how you represent your family when you're going about your day, and having a good sense of humor . . . strong family ties and a close bond between your Native communities."[18]

A Potawatomi participant explained that this sense of community was one fundamental aspect of being a Native person. He stated:

> To me, it means I'm part of a community that's bigger than myself. Being part of that community has responsibilities and benefits, and I think (of) those responsibilities as maintaining our traditional ways and language. And I think also being involved in the community. That's hard sometimes for people, but to me that's what it means to be Potawatomi. It means to be participatory in the community, being recognized by the community that you belong there, and that you do what you can to stay plugged in. That's what it means to be Potawatomi to me.[19]

A Yupik participant echoed this when he stated that everyone in his culture influenced his identity. He explained, "Our elders tell us that we are being influenced by everyone from the time we are born. Even if they are a stranger and they are Yupik, if they are an elder and if they tell you to help them out, you gotta drop what you are doing and help them out. And they would speak to you even if they don't know you. That is kind of like saying, oh I care for you and if you're someone in our culture and our culture needs to be stronger. . . . That is the saying of most of the elders."[20]

While grandparents served an important instructional and encouraging role for participants' spiritual journeys, many also cited traditional healers as influences on their identity. For many Indigenous communities, spiritual leaders and healers are viewed as central members of their communities as keepers of traditional knowledges and practices, connections to other-than-human persons, and are treated with the utmost respect (Deloria 2006; White Hat and Cunnigham 2012). As such, traditional healers and medicine peoples are frequently cited as role models whose examples one could follow as a way to live life. According to one participant, "Growing up over the years, I met several different medicine men, medicine people in general, who really carried themselves with this aura of, of importance, just . . . real dignified, and those were the guys that influenced my life. Not that I wanted to try to be or act like them, but they were the perfect role model of what I would love to have been."[21]

Another participant commented that it was medicine people who taught her about the Red Road and the proper way to live. She said, "The holy people, the medicine people, because they taught me a lot about the knowledge of the spiritual ways and how to walk the path of the Red Road, and a lot of it kind of combines because you go to one tribe and you kind of learn some of the things that you learned in your own. So, I guess it's mostly the spiritual, religious people."[22] These individuals were not just seen as role models, but as teachers. One Ojibwe participant explained, "We have a spiritual advisor here on the reservation . . . and I have really been participating a lot in the ceremonies and stuff that he does, but earlier it was just talking with elders, medicine men, herbalists that we have here on the reservation, and also in other Ojibwe reservations, like up in Canada. I sought out a lot of that stuff and that's what kind of draws me more to our cultural beliefs."[23] A participant from the Great Lakes stated it was a healer from a California tribal community that influenced her through helping her navigate a difficult time in her life. She said, "A healer in southern California . . . took me in and fixed me up and helped me out. He helped me through a healing process, helped me just to discover my identity . . . put me through a couple of fasts . . . he believed in me."[24]

While the majority of participants cited individuals they knew personally, others pointed to the importance of well-known or famous Native peoples who specifically affected them and their identities. Some of these included Native activists, local leaders, and authors. One participant stated that John Trudell, the Santee Dakota activist, was a significant influence on his identity. He stated, "When I was 18, I met John Trudell . . . and he's been a great mentor and a big help. Kind of steering me more into a bigger, more holistic picture of American Indian people. . . . Not just political, but . . . the spiritual, the familial, the nation. He's been a big influence."[25] A participant from the Northwest Coast stated Vine Deloria Jr. influenced him and his identity. He explained:

Vine Deloria, Jr. . . . His way of talking about American Indians is one where we are a complex and intellectual people, and that was the first 'mainstream' author . . . that was speaking to me about who I was in a way that wasn't the stereotypical media way of the dominant society seeing us. . . . I began to see Indian people as more complex than what was portrayed to me as a child, you know . . . he was a real good touchstone for me and kind of allowed me to understand how I was different from everyone else that I was around.[26]

For a few participants, local leaders and activists were also cited as being influences. One participant said it was a local Native from a different tribe who came and visited her school when she was younger. She commented:

> I would say the person who influenced me most was a gentleman named Howard; he's Pueblo. . . . As a young adult I was trying to understand my identity and what my role in society was, whether that be on the reservation or whether that be in an urban setting. I was still trying to figure all those things out through high school. And Howard, he does a lot of youth engagements and him coming to speak at a particular event really inspired me because he wasn't afraid to be proud of who he was as Pueblo, as a Native person. And he really emphasized how important it is to practice prayer and I mean in mainstream, the mainstream communities, especially in our schools, they say we need to separate religions with schools, but as a Native person we're always taught to be spiritual, so we're really unable to do that. We can't distinguish the difference really between that because it's essentially who we are and everything that we do. For him to come out and say be proud of who you are, pray every day, had a profound and lasting influence on who I am today.[27]

Native voices on the Internet have allowed participants to be influenced by other American Indians who might not otherwise have been known and allowed greater connectivity with family members and tribal members. The value of Internet connections in Native communities has been evidenced through its use in contemporary Indigenous activist movements (Johnson 2017), reproducing social relations in disparate Indigenous communities (Virtanen 2015), and opportunities to present Indigenous identities to a wide audience (Rice et al. 2016). This was reflected in conversations with *Native 24/7* participants as well. Social media were seen by some as a means of connection to distant communities and relatives, as well as a way to learn from other community members. One participant from the Northwest stated that his family came from the Southern Plains originally, and that the Internet has allowed him to keep in contact with his tribal community. He explained:

> I got most of the stories of our family from my grandfather. He was the last person in our family to grow up near our reservation; in that vicinity. So, he had the most experiences to share and pass down. . . . Obviously that's important because that's where I got a lot of my family information directly from. Of course, my dad has information, too, but growing up out here in the Pacific Northwest, he also kind of had that, I guess you call it location separation, the same that I do. So, definitely knowing and being able to talk to family members that grew up back east and experience that has been important and just being

able to learn about the history. I keep tabs on my tribe. The Internet is an amazing thing, so I can keep tabs about what's going on locally with the tribe, the tribal government, and the decisions that are being made. There's even cultural and different things you can participate in and learn the language and things like that. . . . Having such available information with technology . . . helps especially if you're not reservation based, which of course is us.[28]

Another participant explained, "Oddly enough, I joined a language group on Facebook and I've been trying to learn to speak and befriended an elder from, not from my tribe, but from a similar tribe, and I email her questions and she gives me good answers and guidance."[29]

Ancestral Connections

In addition to important interpersonal relationships described by participants in the context of their identities, for some participants, influences expanded beyond relationships with other people and extended to the land or, more specifically, ancestral ties to the land. Though small in number (8% of participants), individuals who spoke about ancestral ties to the land discussed it as very important to them. These individuals tended to be from the Great Lakes area, were younger, and were more likely to be female and of mixed heritage. These participants' discussion of ties to the land reflects many scholarly critiques of the category of identity as too focused on the individual and people surrounding the individual. These scholars suggest that greater attention should be paid to environmental circumstances, among others (Alfred and Corntassel 2005). As such, connections to ancestral lands, decolonized diets, and histories are other ways that Indigenous peoples can both understand and practice their identities (Alfred and Corntassel 2005; Weaver 2001; Basso 1996).

Many participants, including not only those who talked about the land or environment directly, described one of the key characteristics of being American Indian as being descended from the "First People" of the Americas. This idea generated a sense of pride for participants and, as such, was central to their identity. Some participants explained it further, as exemplified by one participant as "a deep connection to this place that stretched back forever essentially."[30] In this case, being one of the First Americans established a stronger relationship to the Americas for Native people over and above any other group. This was seen not as a simple issue of land tenure, but more as a relationship to the environments of North America.

Another participant explained the relationship by saying, "The way of life here . . . if we take care of the land, the land will take care of us; it has so much to offer. . . . It's just a continuing education almost every trip out of the house, out into the woods, out on the water. It's a big symbiotic relationship there."[31] Another participant felt that he had a tie to the land and that tie connected him to Creator. He commented, "It means that I'm unique, and that I have a blood tie to this land. . . . It means that I understand my place on this Earth. It means that I have a specific and distinct responsibility to take care of this land along with the understanding of our relationship with *Wakonda*, or God."[32]

A Navajo participant tied this connection to the land to her ancestors, "It would be my late grandparents. They were traditional and lived in a very rural area, so we relied a lot on just the land and the animals. With that it gave us a sense of connection with the place and everything had a purpose. My grandparents were very, very traditional and were involved with ceremony and prayer and they taught us a lot with just being Navajo."[33]

For some participants, having an ancestral background that originated in North America also extended beyond relationships with the environment in a broad sense to include specific locations in the landscape that are culturally or historically significant to their communities. One participant explained that she and her whole community had a responsibility to care for the lake on her reservation. She said that her identity was linked to "a strong sense of family, a connectedness to our land, our lake. Our reservation is held in trust, so we are all equally responsible for our land, our water, its environment. It's a feeling you have. The lake feeds our people; we all take care of the lake."[34]

One participant stated, "Being American Indian to me . . . (is) a sense of pride because we are the first nations, we are the first inhabitants of Turtle Island, so that's what brings me a lot of pride . . . we're the ones that were here first."[35] With that came a connection to the land for many participants. An elder from the Great Lakes stated, "This is our homeland. We are a part of this earth . . . the soil in North America."[36] Another participant explained that "being Native American means I can look back and feel a really strong connection with my ancestors. I love the sense of that when I'm home, I know that our people have lived in that area forever and it gives me an incredible amount of strength and pride, and a sense of belonging and feeling like if everything else is going haywire I can always go back to that land."[37]

A Haida participant went as far back as the beginning of time, explaining that his people have been on the land since the beginning of time. He said:

> It gives me a sense of pride knowing that I can trace my history back to the beginning of . . . time. We always talk about it (time) immemorial. . . . They always ask us how long we've been here? Our grandmas say forever . . . we've

been here since the beginning of time. You know, us Haidas, we trace it back to you know . . . the Ice Age. We have stories of ice coming down the river. Those Arapahos, they're the same way; they have their stories of the Ice Age and they weathered it out. . . . It gives me a sense of pride to know that we've been here.[38]

In many cases these ideas of community coalesce around connections to specific places in the landscape and make these connections an essential factor in understanding oneself and one's community. This may lead to the idea that it is about being in a reservation community on traditional lands. However, the majority of reservations are not located on the traditional lands of the people who live there. This suggests that the connection goes beyond where an individual is currently living. This is further exemplified by the fact that, in some cases, the individuals talking about connection to land were not even from reservation communities. An Oneida participant who grew up in an urban area stated that he was proud of being one of the original land owners. He explained:

Being Oneida, to me, is being unique; being one of the first nations of this country, first land owners. As Oneida people we are descendants of the long necks. Our major clans being Turtle, Bear, and Wolf. Makes us identify who we are with this land and our connection to this land. Being Oneida is being the original land owners. Being proud of who we are, where we come from. You know we live our life which has endured many years of assimilation. Being Oneida first is being unique and being authentic to what the White society thinks we are now.[39]

For some participants this connection to the land was described as a spiritual relationship that was in contrast to the environmental exploitation of many people in mainstream America. One participant explained that this relationship set Native peoples apart from others because "the way we see the world, that we're not supposed to take from the earth without giving back . . . or asking for things through prayer . . . or asking permission."[40]

Participants also discussed feeling a strong connection to the history of Indigenous peoples in North America as an extension of their own blood-related ancestors, again showing the influence of Native people and community outside of their nuclear family on their identity. For one participant from a Northeastern urban community this was a central tenet of being Native. She stated that "it's just living a certain way of life that is in accordance with my ancestors and my family and my community. . . . There's definite connections to the homelands. . . . There's a lot of history steeped in where we live and how we've lived for a very long period of time. . . . They shaped a lot of the beliefs and foundations I developed as a child. I've been really firm in who I was because of community support and just learning about my culture and my ancestors."[41] Another participant explained, "Knowing that my ancestors have lived here forever; knowing that I am connected to this land, this place . . . knowing that I have a huge family to take care of me"[42] defined what being Indian meant to her. Many participants understood their continued practice of Indigenous cultures was one way that they could both connect to their ancestors and express their identities concurrently. This discussion also included recognition of the struggles of important figures in Native American history for some participants. One participant focused on the Chiricahua Apache leader Geronimo as an influence on his identity, saying, "Geronimo. I like him as an idol. He fought right to the last to keep the land and everything."[43]

Connection to ancestors was only a part of the picture; connection to descendants came up in conversations as well. Participants thought not only about their actions being drawn from their North American ancestors, but also how their actions impacted future generations. One participant stated that being Indian "means that I am connected to all those that came before me and that the way that I choose to walk in my life will affect the seven generations in front of me. So, when it comes to being connected to my culture I am very mindful of what I reach out to, what I do, how I act, the things that I say. So, being American Indian has a lot to do with just who I am."[44]

Conclusion

A simplistic interpretation of the views of Native 24/7 participants would say that Indigenous peoples draw heavily on their family members to both support and learn about their identities. This is only part of the story. A more focused understanding of these findings reveals that it is necessary to understand what it means to be a family member or community member in many Native communities and how relatedness can be from more than blood relationships.

As the conversations with Native 24/7 participants revealed, connections to family and community members, as well as ancestors and ancestral lands are significant influences of how American Indian peoples construct and understand their identities. However, unlike the views of many people from mainstream communities across the United States, Native conceptions of family and relationships to community are often more complex and reflect the importance of a wider variety of familial and community influences.

Notes

1. 28-year-old male from a Southern Plains rural community.
2. 54-year-old female from a Northern Plains reservation community.
3. 23-year-old male from a Northeastern urban community.
4. 29-year-old male from a Northern Plains reservation community.
5. 26-year-old male from a Northern Plains rural community.
6. 36-year-old female from a Southeastern rural community.
7. 45-year-old male from a Plateau reservation community.
8. 30-year-old female from Great Basin reservation community.
9. 48-year-old female from a Southwestern reservation community.
10. 35-year-old female from a Northern Plains rural community.
11. 20-year-old male from a Northern Plains rural community.
12. 43-year-old male from a Great Basin rural community.
13. 19-year-old female from a Southwestern rural community.
14. The Dakota 38 refers to thirty-eight Dakota men and boys who were executed on December 26, 1862 in Mankato, Minnesota, for their supposed and now questioned participation in the US-Dakota War of 1862. This represents the largest mass execution in US history.
15. 24-year-old male from a Northern Plains urban community.
16. 24-year-old female from a Great Basin rural community.
17. 38-year-old male from a Southern Plains urban community.
18. 26-year-old male from a California urban community.
19. 43-year-old male from a Southern Plains rural community.
20. 23-year-old male from an Artic rural community.
21. 48-year-old male from a Northern Plains rural community.
22. 61-year-old female from a Northern Plains rural community.
23. 42-year-old female from a Great Lakes reservation community.
24. 47-year-old female from a Great Lakes reservation community.
25. 45-year-old male from a Southeastern rural community.
26. 43-year-old male participant from a Northwest Coast urban community.
27. 25-year-old female participant from a Plateau reservation community.
28. 43-year-old male from a Northwest urban community.
29. 40-year-old female from a Great Lakes urban community.
30. 26-year-old male from a Southern Plains reservation community.
31. 52-year-old male from a Northwest Coast reservation community.
32. 27-year-old male from a Southern Plains rural community.
33. 29-year-old female from a Southwestern rural community.
34. 59-year-old female from a Great Lakes reservation community.
35. 46-year-old male from a Plateau reservation community.
36. 76-year-old female from a Great Lakes reservation community.
37. 46-year-old female from a Southwestern rural community.
38. 45-year-old male from a Plateau reservation community.

39. 46-year-old male from a Southern Plains urban community.
40. 34-year-old male from a Southern Plains reservation community.
41. 26-year-old female from a Northeast urban community.
42. 26-year-old female from a Great Lakes urban community.
43. 51-year-old male from a Great Lakes reservation community.
44. 34-year-old female from a Great Lakes urban community.

CHAPTER FIVE

~

"I'm Only Indian on Sunday"

Religion and Spirituality

The religious and spiritual landscape of Native America is complex, varied, and increasingly diverse. To some degree this has always been true given the impressive level of cultural diversity within the Americas producing nearly as many unique religious and spiritual traditions as there were communities before the arrival of Europeans. The imposition, adoption, and integration of Christianity within Native communities, beginning almost in tandem with the arrival of colonists, further set the stage for the context we see today. Like many communities around the world, Indigenous peoples hold religious and spiritual beliefs as highly influential structures and practices that promote an understanding of themselves within their environments (Martin 2001). This can be seen in the ways that Indigenous religious and spiritual practices are engrained in historical and contemporary activist movements (DeMallie 1982; Goeckner et al. 2020) and language revitalization movements (Davis 2015).

This has also been true in health programming for Native peoples, particularly in the realm of substance abuse. For example, successful smoking-cessation programs in American Indian communities portray tobacco as sacred and worthy of respect, rather than denote it as "evil," which is the case in many mainstream quit smoking programs (Daley, James et al. 2006; Daley, Greiner et al. 2010). The Red Road to Wellbriety, one of the more successful alcohol treatment programs in Native communities, is a modification of the Alcoholics Anonymous (AA) program based on Native spirituality (White Bison 2002). With this importance given to religion and spirituality in mind, *Native 24/7* participants were asked to discuss the ways in which religion and spirituality were influential in their lives and how this, in turn, impacted their understandings of themselves as Indigenous peoples.

Much like Indigenous identities in the United States, contemporary religious and spiritual practices in Native communities are plagued by a complicated history of policy, legislated or otherwise, external affronts to self-determination, and the continuation of colonialism (Irwin 1997). The role played by Christianity in Native America is pointedly summed up by Lakota scholar Vine Deloria Jr. (1969), "When they arrived, they had only the Book and we had the land; now we have the Book and they have the land" (101). Some scholars argue that the history of settler colonialism in the Americas was directly a consequence of religious zeal sparked by the Roman Catholic Church's Doctrine of Discovery in 1493 providing apparent justification for the wholesale seizure of lands from non-Christians around the world (Deloria 1973).

After the establishment of the United States federal government, attempts to erase Indigenous existence within the new republic continued to focus on religious conversion as one of the key methods to deal with the "Indian problem." Mirroring the early establishment of praying Indian towns in colonial New England (Brenner 1980), the attempted erasure of Indigenous religious and spiritual traditions via European religion continued well into the twentieth century (Irwin 1997). Put infamously by Lieutenant Richard Henry Pratt, the goal of assimilationist policies exercised through boarding school education, often administered by religious authorities, was to "kill the Indian, save the man" (Peterson 2013). Conversion was seen as a clear means to assimilate Native peoples into mainstream American culture, and religious organizations were paid to run such schools (Colmant 2000).

Despite this tragic historical context, Indigenous religions and spiritualities in the United States have not been erased. *Native 24/7* participants revealed that religion and spirituality, including both Native and non-Native, as well as a combination of spiritualities, remain centrally important facets of their lives for understanding themselves as Indigenous peoples broadly and as members of their specific communities. For many Native peoples, religious identity can be understood as a network of social relations beyond other human community members to include relationships to place, significant objects, animals, and spiritual beings and forces (Gooding 1996).

Like contemporary Native identity, Native religions and spiritualities are frequently complicated by questions of authenticity by both scholars and Native peoples themselves. This association with being authentically American Indian and practicing Native religious and spiritual traditions was character-ized by one *Native 24/7* participant who explained, "Some of my elders think we should believe in [Native] tradition and how we weren't created by God, we were created by our own God. . . . We should follow by what traditions the Native Americans had instead of being Baptist or Christian or anything like that."[1] Further, the romanticization of Native peoples has not only lead to wanton appropriation of Native spiritual traditions, but also emboldened inaccurate stereotypes that paint Indigenous communities as overly spiritual and unchanged since before the arrival of Europeans in the Americas (Aldred 2000). Native people have not stayed locked in a particular moment in time, but have continued to incorporate new ideas and practices into their spirituality like all other people. They continue to practice their traditional religions and spiritual traditions, bringing in new ideas as cultures change, and actively use religious and spiritual beliefs and activities to denote community belonging and to identify who is or is not a part of their community.

Many *Native 24/7* participants believed that their individual religious and spiritual practices were important markers of their membership within American Indian communities; 56 percent of participants who answered the question about religion or spirituality named it as influential in their identity as Native people. The vast majority of these individuals (97%) said that this was a positive influence on their identity. One participant noted, "Native Americans are spiritual people . . . and without spirituality, where would we be? That is essentially part of who we are."[2] Many participants explained that this was one important defining characteristic about being Indigenous. One participant explained, "What sets us apart is our connection with our culture and our ceremonies that we do, trying to be one with the universe and other things here on Earth."[3]

However seemingly simple these statements of religious and spiritual belonging may seem, conversations with *Native 24/7* participants revealed a much more nuanced picture of Indigenous religious and spiritual beliefs and practices. This is particularly true when considering differential definitions of religion and spirituality, the prevalence of multiple religious belonging and plurality in Native America, and the overall importance of relationships in understanding American Indian religious and spiritual identities.

Native Theologies

Much discussion among anthropologists, religious studies scholars, sociologists, and others in the social sciences and humanities surrounds the problem of defining conceptual categories, such as religion, with which we divide the world (Murphy 2017; Orsi 2010; Orsi 2006; Van Niekerk 2018;

Zinnbauer et al. 1997). Western scientific thought is often premised on the idea that individual facets of society can be isolated for study, requiring clearly bounded criteria to differentiate one from the other. Academic debate over the subtle differences between disciplinary or individual definitions of terms like "religion" and "spirituality" is constant and largely theoretical, lacking clear ties to application in real life or how everyday people talk. Defining what does and does not qualify as religion has, historically, shifted based on a number of factors influencing the disciplinary exclusivity of the concept (Chidester 2014; Masuzawa 2005; Smith 1998). However, academic opinions about these differences are largely lacking the viewpoints of individuals from underrepresented communities. Although exceptions exist (Taylor and Chatters 2010), opinions among American Indians are particularly lacking in the academic literature. Public discussion of differences among these terms is lacking as well, with the terms often used interchangeably or without explanation for why that term was selected. Although not a primary purpose in *Native 24/7*, interviews revealed strong differences among participants about what constitutes these related, but often contested, concepts.

Participants were asked if religion or spirituality had an influence on their identity. In addition to naming it as influential or not, many participants discussed the distinction between these two concepts, particularly in the context of Native America. Many *Native 24/7* participants described their understanding of religion as being primarily Christian, while spirituality was seen as mainly the Native approach to beliefs and a way of life. One *Native 24/7* participant stated, "I guess when people say religion, I think of organized religion such as church and stuff. . . . Spirituality is more personal."[4] Another participant explained it by saying, "American Indian, if you want to call them religions, and they are organized, they are, they're not institutions in the sense, say like Christian churches. . . . So, I think that they (Native ways) are in more of a spiritual sense than a religious sense, you know, but they certainly are religious."[5]

Formal organization did not seem to play into participants' differentiations between religion and spirituality, for the most part, as there are organized characteristics within Native spiritualities that hold importance. For example, it would be difficult to discuss Diné spiritual health diagnostic practices (e.g., hand trembling) and songs or ceremonials as lacking organization or institution. *Hataali*, or singers, and *ndilniihii*, or hand tremblers, are part of a highly organized system wherein an individual who is out of *hozhó*, or balance, is first diagnosed, then sent to an appropriate singer to perform a specific curing ceremonial with intricate detail that must be done in a certain and, often, at a certain time of year (Levy, Neutra, and Parker 1988). This is similar to Western medical practices of diagnostics and referrals to specialty care or, in Roman Catholic spiritual healing, identification of individuals suffering from possession who are then referred to exorcists to perform a highly ritualized and organized ceremony (Amorth 1999).

Participants also suggested that religion, in their experiences, is somewhat superficial and separated from everyday life. A Lakota participant explained,

> You know, living in the Lakota way of life is living a spiritual life. It's not just at Sundance four days of the year . . . or one ceremony or one sweat or some type of ceremony that you might attend. It's all day, every day, twenty-four-seven. It's a way to live, it's a way of life and to me, that's spirituality . . . whereas religion is oftentimes a set of rules and regulations, and meeting times in places that are a little constricted, a little bit more organized and formal. Where ours is literally a way of life, and you can't separate our spirituality and our culture . . . they are one and the same.[6]

Describing the difference between religion and spirituality as it relates to their practices, one participant stated, "I do not believe in religion because religion is only practiced one day a week; Sundays, sometimes Thursdays or Wednesdays or Tuesdays, but most of them are only practiced on Sundays. To me, spirituality . . . is a strong gift . . . a strong way of life . . . but spirituality it is not a religion, it is a way of life."[7] This notion was repeated by several participants, including one Navajo participant who explained the contrast between Christianity and Native spiritual traditions. She explained:

> I realized that . . . people are only Christian on Sundays, but they weren't the rest of the week. . . . I'm Navajo every day of the week so, you know, I don't have the ability to be like, well I'm only Navajo on Sunday, when I go in and repent and pray and all that. . . . I think by realizing that, I didn't want to take part in like Christianity religions because it was just, well, it kind of seemed fake to me. . . . Being Navajo . . . our taboos and all of our stories and language and everything, it was every day of the week.[8]

These statements illustrate a distinction that religion is Christian and spirituality is Native. They also showcase a potentially negative view of religion, specifically Christianity. It is possible that these views are tied to proselytization, forced conversions, and religious boarding schools, as well US federal laws and policies based in Christian thought and ethics. Though not always created by leaders in Christian Churches, often these policies were seen as a part of the Christian religions whose members were leading boarding schools and held the majority of political offices, thus driving laws and policies. This may help to explain the *Native 24/7* participants, albeit a small number (eleven people), who said that religion or spirituality had a negative influence on their identity. It may also help to explain the 44 percent of participants who said that religion or spirituality had no influence on their identity. This view may be backlash from boarding schools and other US federal policies entrenched in Christianity. Some participants may have only been thinking about Christianity when asked the question about religion and spirituality and, thus, wanted to make it clear that Christianity did not influence their identity.

Native 24/7 participants felt a stronger connection to what they termed as spiritual, rather than religious, beliefs and practices, often drawing a contrast between religion (Christianity) and Indigenous spiritual traditions. Many participants viewed spirituality as lived and highly practical, "a way of life"[9] constructed through "personal"[10] experience and community. Arguing that spirituality is essential to being Native, one participant explained, "That's part of who you are and it's part of your everyday life. It's not just something that you do on a certain day or time."[11] The idea was that everyday existence was imbued with spirituality and inescapable for many community members. One participant noted, "Spirituality, for us (Native peoples) isn't really looked at as religion; like there's no actual name for it, as opposed to somebody who's Christian or Baptist. We just follow spirituality. So, I think it gives us a different perspective of how we live our lives and how we look at things."[12]

In describing the difference between religion and spirituality, some participants argued that religion does not exist within American Indian communities. One participant noted, "I believe that being Native American, that it is important to be spiritual, and that each individual or each tribe, or each individual Native American, has their own views on spirituality, but as for religion, [it] is not a term that I would use with Native Americans."[13] According to a Navajo elder, religion is a non-Native concept. When asked if religion or spirituality influenced her and her identity, she explained,

> Yes, it does, my spirituality. I wouldn't quite say religion again, that's another White man term and their view of what religion is, is very narrow, very centered as to what they want, you know, other people to believe. And a lot of them force those views, and so to me, religion and spirituality are two separate things. And I would say that I have spirituality. . . . I guess religion is a way to express how to, for them anyway, that's what I think that's their life, you know, to belong to a church, like a Catholic church or a Mormon church or whatever, you know? That's a religion.[14]

Another participant stated that religion was understood to be inadequate for explaining the integration of spiritual belief and practice within Indigenous worldviews. "Being Native American is my identity. . . . I don't need religion because I have spirituality because I'm Native American and I have . . . a Native path. . . . I don't necessarily agree with organized religion. . . . I think there's more to it than that."[15] One participant even drew upon linguistic evidence by saying, "Spirituality, for us, isn't really looked at as a religion. Like there's no actual name for it. So, I think it gives us a different perspective of how we live our lives and how we look at things"[16] This lack of a word for "religion," particularly in Indigenous communities, has been widely documented by missionaries and scholars.

This distinction was further supported by the fact that some participants appeared to contradict themselves throughout their interviews. When asked directly about the impact of religion and spirituality on their identities, 35 percent initially replied that it, religion, was not an important factor in their lives. However, throughout the rest of the interview, a portion of these individuals (22% of those who initially said that it was not important) revealed that it was in fact influential by explaining the importance of participating in ceremonies and living a life in accordance with their communities' worldviews and spiritual traditions. One clear example of this is a participant who stated, "There are other cultures that have their own religions and they are spiritual and stuff like that, but ours is based on our beliefs and it includes the land and stuff, too. So, I think that sets us apart because we are one with nature and animals and stuff like that."[17] But, when asked directly about the influence of religion and spirituality upon his understanding of himself, this participant stated that neither was important to his identity. Other *Native 24/7* participants responded similarly.

The changing views of participants may be partially a consequence of the question's wording—"Does religion or spirituality affect your view of your identity?"—combined with the overall history of organized religion in Native communities. Many participants addressed the differences between religion and spirituality, explaining first how religion was not always applicable to Indigenous communities, followed by their definition and experience practicing Native spiritual traditions. The frequent negative connotation attributed to non-Native religions suggests that participants may have simply reacted to the first part of the question without fully considering how religion and spirituality can be understood differently.

Plurality in Native America

Despite many participants' strongly held conviction that the differences between religion and spirituality are central for understanding the theological landscape of Native America, a large number of them discussed not exclusively adhering to one tradition or another. Only some participants identified their religion or spiritual belief system (318 participants, 66%). Among those who did, 68 percent identified as ascribing to their tribe's spiritual beliefs and practices or "Native spirituality"; an additional 4 percent specified belonging to the Native American Church. Twenty-six percent of these individuals identified as Christian of some type, and the remaining 2 percent identified other religious traditions. Other participants did not specify their belief system. Even among those who identified a specific religious tradition, there was much discussion of incorporating other beliefs and practices in their lives.

Described as multiple religious belonging, this framework has been used to explain a variety of circumstances by religious studies scholars and theologians (Cornille 2010; Phan 2003; Roberts 2010; Gustafson 2016). In contrast to syncretism, where elements of two separate traditions are merged together to produce something new, multiple religious belonging seeks to explain the way that individuals are able to practice two traditions without "violat[ing] the unique identity of each religion" (Phan 2003). Primarily, scholars have applied this to Christian belief and practice beyond the scope of Christianity. Although not an apparent problem for many religions around the world, among the Abrahamic faiths (the various forms of Judaism, Christianity, and Islam), whose adherents presume to offer singular truth, the incorporation of other religious beliefs and practices has historically been problematic. Largely a consequence of experiences between Europeans with adherents of Asian religious traditions such as Buddhism, Confucianism, Shinto, or Hinduism, theologians have endeavored to explain how individuals can remain true Christians while adhering to seemingly conflicting beliefs (Cornille 2010; Phan 2003; Van Bragt 2010). This has been particularly true in its application in American Indian contexts (Gustafson 2016; Stoeber 2020; Stolzman 1991).

Removed from a theological debate, however, this approach is useful for understanding the present context of American Indian spirituality. While missionaries and the United States federal government sought to replace Indigenous religious and spiritual traditions with various forms of Christianity, *Native 24/7* participants suggested that they may have simply offered American Indian peoples practices and beliefs to supplement those that already existed in their communities. Although instances of syncretism within Native communities certainly resulted from these interactions—for example, the Native American Church is a combination of Christianity and multiple different Native beliefs—*Native 24/7*'s findings suggest that the pluralistic environment of American Indian religions and spirituality gives rise to an openness particularly amenable to multiple religious belonging.

While many participants expressed a stronger connection to Indigenous spiritual traditions, some described a sense of multiple religious belonging that included Native traditions alongside a number of Christian faiths. These individuals described their spiritual practice as drawing upon both Native traditions and various Christian denominations. One participant explained, "Everyone believes in someone much higher than us, and that's the Creator, no matter what religion it is. . . . I can believe in some ways in the Christian churches and I can believe in some ways in Native American churches."[18] Another participant explained, "I still have both. I have my Native heritage and my normal religion and it doesn't really conflict."[19] It is unclear, however, what was meant by "normal religion."

Overall, *Native 24/7* participants mentioned a variety of Christian denominations and faiths including Roman Catholicism, The Church of Jesus Christ of Latter-day Saints (Mormons), and numerous Protestant denominations in terms of religions they either practiced or to which they had been exposed. Regardless of the denomination, participants consistently talked about the incorporation of both their Christian religion and their Native spirituality into their lives. Although never explicitly asked, many participants relied on this identification as a means to describe their relationship to the concepts of religion and spirituality within their interview. Many participants described the influence of Catholicism upon their identity and religious and spiritual beliefs and practices. One such participant explained, "I'm a spiritual person because I am Native American, but at the same time I do follow the Catholic religion."[20] One Church of Jesus Christ of Latter-day Saints participant described his practice by saying, "(I) still integrate a lot of both teachings and values of the Navajo culture into what I do on a daily basis."[21] Although something of an outlier amongst participants, one *Native 24/7* participant identified as Buddhist. She explained, "I'm Buddhist. So, Buddhism kind of ties to my Native American culture. It kind of connects; like what they believe . . . you, know, to be kind to one another, and things like that."[22]

There were also many participants who described growing up with one tradition, typically a form of Christianity, and then learning about and becoming more involved with another, typically their Native spirituality, later in life. One participant explained, "I was raised with religion, but the more I got older when I went off to school, I just kind of started paying attention to my Lakota side. Religion, honestly, we all pray to the same person. We all pray to *Tunkasila*, it's just a different set of rules different people made, so, it just felt more at home with me to go back to my spirituality and traditional ways than religion."[23] Another participant described a singular experience that prompted this change by saying, "We were raised to be strict Catholics and then I left the Church when I was 13. And the first time I ever went into a prayer meeting, or a meeting with the drum, it was like I came home. You could smell the sage and just talking to Grandfather, it was just spirituality."[24]

The propensity for multiple religious belonging suggests some things about religion and spirituality among contemporary Native peoples. First, the cultural and spiritual diversity among American Indian communities creates opportunities for many Native people to be exposed to and learn about a variety of spiritual traditions beyond those practiced in their home communities. As noted by one participant, "Every tribe has, like, their own creation stories and they have their own ceremonies and their own song and dance and everything's just unique to them."[25] This lack of exclusivity may create a perspective where no single religion is believed to represent complete truth, but rather, all spiritual and religious traditions hold some validity, at least as it was explained described by many of our participants. While many participants expressed an affinity for their own community's spiritual traditions, there was little antagonism toward other faiths. The openness resulting from this pluralistic environment where "each tribe or each individual Native American has their own views on spirituality"[26] may help explain the acceptance of Pan-Indianism among some Native peoples and communities (Paper 1988).

This also may suggest that federal governmental efforts to erase Indigenous ways of life that targeted Indigenous religions and spiritualities often were largely unsuccessful. Despite the relative success of these efforts in some cases, it would appear that contemporary American Indian communities are and were accepting of a variety of faiths. As such, missionary efforts to replace Indigenous spiritualities with various Christian faiths were thwarted by the nature of Indigenous religious perspectives. The plurality of belief in the Americas prior to and since the arrival of Europeans, combined with an openness toward other belief systems, created an environment in which Christian faiths were often seen as complementary rather than opposed to Indigenous religious and spiritual traditions. Although the damage wrought by assimilationist policies and boarding schools should not be understated, based on conversations with *Native 24/7* participants, it seems that this perspective is still strong today.

Practicing multiple religions was supported in some communities through attempts by religious authorities to make Christian faiths more palatable and relevant to Indigenous peoples. One key example of this comes from Jesuit missionaries' efforts to spread Catholic belief among Lakota communities by integrating Lakota worldviews and spiritual figures into their teachings (Steinmetz 1998; Stolzman 1991). Examples of integration of Christian beliefs and practices into Indigenous religions and spiritualities number nearly as high as the number of communities themselves. The integration of Catholic Feast Days among Pueblo communities in the Southwest (Mc-Comb Sanchez 2020) and the widespread practice of the syncretic Native American Church (Stewart 1987) are just some of the numerous examples that could be cited for this intermingling of faiths.

This perspective contributes to the long-standing debate amongst scholars about the true nature of Nicholas Black Elk's religiosity as both a Lakota medicine man and Catholic convert. Questions of whether his visionary experiences, detailed in Neihardt's *Black Elk Speaks*, represent an "authentic" Lakota spiritual perspective at such a tumultuous time in Lakota history have led many to suggest he may have been too heavily influenced by his Catholic conversion nearly thirty years before his work with Neihardt (Neihardt 1996). As some scholars have suggested, Black Elk may have practiced what Bhabha (1985) describes as a hybridity, evidencing something of a negotiation between the two traditions (Bhabha 1985; Stoeber 2020). This was expressed by one of our participants who explained, "I was raised Catholic and I still kept my traditions and sometimes I follow both and it's the best of two worlds. . . . As Catholics . . . even at ceremonies, we sing Amazing Grace, but it's in our Native language."[27]

While the above may be true, based on interviews with *Native 24/7* participants it seems that this may be less a question of differential power dynamics within a colonial encounter and more of an expression of the theological approach that many American Indians appear to have practiced historically and presently. Although colonialism cannot be discounted, this conclusion suggests a stronger sense of agency amongst American Indian peoples, who had some power in determining in which religious and spiritual practices they would participate.

Religion, Spirituality, and Relationships

For many *Native 24/7* participants, relationships were often a motivating factor for involvement and interest in religious or spiritual traditions. While family and community members were described generally as being highly influential, this was particularly true in the context of religious and spiritual beliefs and practices. Regardless of religious or spiritual affiliation, participants frequently discussed the importance of these individuals in informing their own beliefs. In describing his spiritual practice, one participant emphasized that "we have spirituality . . . in our beliefs that I grew up with. . . . My grandmother was a healer in the tribe, and my other grandmother was a *yupta* in our tribe which is a . . . dreamer, spiritual leader. . . . We had our own beliefs . . . not the Bible."[28] This importance was also frequently described as a major mechanism for the continuance of Native spiritual traditions. One participant explained, "We have a strong spirituality that has been handed down from generation to generation . . . family . . . they participated in ceremonies and passed them down to me and taught me the rights and wrongs, and dos and don'ts, and respect. So, I would say that is what kind of made my identity."[29] Another participant noted that an elder from her community had a significant impact on her. She stated, "She was one of the elders here in Michigan. She had a huge impact on me. . . . She was an elder in the community. She was a very strong woman, and she believed in the holy traditional ways, the old ways. It was just that strong thing about her."[30] Another placed this responsibility on herself, saying, "It's important to me how I think about my relations with the world around me, and it's important for my family and for me to teach my child the way that I have learned. It's important that he knows what it means, spiritually, to be Indian."[31]

This connection to family and kin was not only important for living relatives, however. *Native 24/7* participants frequently described the importance of practicing their communities' religious and spiritual traditions as one way that they are able to both honor and feel connected to their ancestors. One participant explained this connection as, "It makes me who I am. . . . We link ourselves to our ancestors and what they all died for, and what they represented. And we try to represent that the way we present ourselves, that's what I try to do anyways."[32] Another participant explained that this was a key factor in differentiating between religion and spirituality. She explained, "I feel more connected to the spiritual aspects of my identity than I do with Christianity. I think both of them have value, but as far as feeling . . . connected to something and feeling that I have ancestors that have done this before me, it's [spirituality] more of a deeper meaning."[33] One participant explained that she felt "well cared for by my elders who passed on."[34] For some participants this was understood in more than a simply metaphorical sense. A Kiowa elder explained, "My ancestors and grandparents were medicine people, people among my tribe which is the Kiowa tribe of Oklahoma. . . . [I'm] able to pray with their pipes, their staffs, their warrior staffs, their tomahawks, their arrows, their horns, the medicine bags that I keep, the medicine bundles that I keep. It's a beautiful honor to walk in my grandfather's tracks."[35]

Differences among *Native 24/7* Participants

Demographic factors had little impact on whether or not religion or spirituality influenced a participant's identity (see table 5.1). Because only eleven total participants said that religion influenced them in a negative way, it is impossible to characterize demographic variables related to negative influence (see figure 5.1). When examining positive influence versus no influence, a few trends begin to emerge, but offer little insight into whether or not someone views religion or spirituality as an influence. Older individuals were more likely to say that religion or spirituality was an influence than younger people. This may reflect the changing views of the importance of religion or spirituality in the general population. Over the past 30+ years, there has been a decline in the United States overall in affiliation with a particular religion, particularly among younger people aged 18–29. In 1986, only 10 percent of younger people (age 18–29) considered themselves unaffiliated with a religious group compared to 3 percent of older people (age 65+). In 2020, these numbers changed to 36 percent of younger people versus 14 percent of older people (Public Religion Research Institution 2021). Higher education

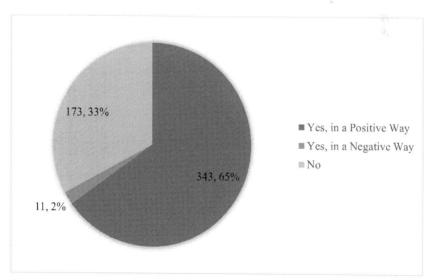

Figure 5.1. Did Religion or Spirituality Influence Your Identity (N=527 mentions by participants). *Credit*: Christine M. Daley, Charley Lewis, and Joseph Pacheco.

Table 5.1. Did Religion or Spirituality Influence Your Identity by Demographic Characteristics

Demographic Characteristic	Yes in a Positive Way N (%)	Yes in a Negative Way N (%)	No N (%)
Gender (N=527)			
Male	140 (41%)	3 (27%)	63 (36%)
Female	203 (59%)	8 (73%)	110 (64%)
Age (N=527)			
18-29	110 (32%)	2 (18%)	65 (38%)
30-49	122 (36%)	7 (64%)	68 (39%)
50+	111 (32%)	2 (18%)	40 (23%)
Marital Status (N=508)			
Married/In a Relationship	178 (53%)	6 (55%)	82 (50%)
Never Married/Divorced/Separated/ Widowed	155 (47%)	5 (45%)	82 (50%)
Children (N=521)			
Yes	228 (67%)	9 (82%)	117 (68%)
No	110 (33%)	2 (18%)	55 (32%)
Education Level (N=521)			
GED or High School	68 (20%)	4 (36%)	72 (42%)
Post-High School Training or 2-year College Degree	138 (41%)	2 (18%)	80 (47%)
4-year College Degree or Higher	132 (39%)	5 (45%)	20 (12%)
Employment Status			
Currently Employed	239 (71%)	11 (100%)	115 (67%)
Not Currently Employed	96 (29%)	0 (0%)	56 (33%)
American Indian Alone or Mixed Race (N=527)			
American Indian	259 (76%)	9 (82%)	140 (81%)
American Indian in Combination with Another Race/Ethnicity	84 (24%)	2 (18%)	33 (19%)
Enrollment Status (N=516)			
Enrolled	273 (81%)	11 (100%)	143 (86%)
Not Enrolled	65 (19%)	0 (0%)	24 (14%)
Area Where Raised (N=523)			
Reservation or Tribal Trust Land	168 (49%)	4 (36%)	104 (60%)
Off-Reservation	172 (51%)	7 (64%)	68 (40%)
Culture Area (N=527)			
California	23 (7%)	1 (9%)	19 (11%)
Great Basin & Plateau	29 (8%)	2 (18%)	17 (10%)
Great Lakes	68 (20%)	4 (36%)	30 (17%)
Northeast & Southeast	36 (11%)	1 (9%)	13 (8%)
Northern Plains	49 (14%)	1 (9%)	45 (26%)
Northwest Coast, Arctic, Subarctic	21 (6%)	1 (9%)	6 (3%)
Southern Plains	72 (21%)	1 (9%)	22 (13%)
Southwest	45 (13%)	0 (0%)	21 (12%)

NOTE: Total N for each demographic variable are different based on whether or not an individual answered the demographic question. Percentages are presented as column percentages. Percentages may not total 100 due to rounding.

Credit: Christine M. Daley, Charley Lewis, and Joseph Pacheco

level and being employed also had some impact on naming religion or spirituality as an influence, though not a strong one.

Individuals enrolled in their tribe or growing up on a reservation or tribal trust land were somewhat less likely to name religion or spirituality as an influence. This was as not a strong trend. No clear trends were present among other demographic variables. It may be that the sample size of *Native 24/7* was too small to pick up on differences by demographic variables or that other factors are more influential than the ones included in this study.

Participants were not asked specifically to name their religious affiliation. However, during the interviews participants who talked about religion or spirituality extemporaneously revealed this information a majority of the time (66% of participants named a particular faith). The remaining participants who talked about religion or spirituality talked in general terms and did not mention a particular affiliation. Among those who named an affiliation, a majority (68%) considered themselves to be a part of either their tribe's religion or spiritual tradition, or Native religion or spirituality. Twenty-six percent named some type of Christianity, 4 percent named the Native American Church, and 2 percent named another organized faith. Figure 5.2 presents religious affiliation of all those who named religion as an influence.

When examined by demographic variable, unclear trends emerged regarding religious affiliation (see table 5.2). Differences were not apparent by

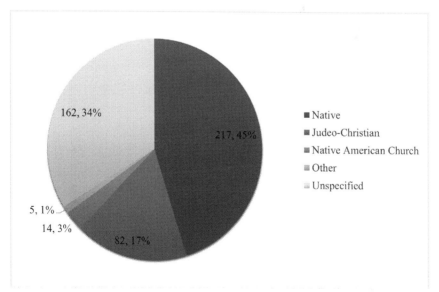

Figure 5.2. Types of Religion Represented by Participants (N=480). *Credit:* **Christine M. Daley, Charley Lewis, and Joseph Pacheco.**

gender, age, or whether or not someone had children. Individuals who were married or in a relationship tended to be more likely to name a Christian religion. People with lower formal educational attainment were less likely to name a particular affiliation, and those with higher formal educational attainment were more likely to both name an affiliation and to name Christianity more specifically. Currently employed participants were more likely to name Christian religions.

People identifying as solely American Indian rather than in combination with another race or ethnicity were slightly more likely to identify as practicing a Native religion or spiritual tradition, though when examined by enrollment status, people who were enrolled were somewhat more likely to name a Christian religion. People who grew up on a reservation or tribal trust land were less likely to name a Christian religion, but not more likely to name a Native religious affiliation. There were no clear trends apparent in area of the country in which an individual was raised. These slight trends do not provide any clear picture of the influence of demographic factors on type of religion among *Native 24/7* participants. Once again, it may be that the sample size was too small to identify differences or that other factors not requested or discussed were more important.

Table 5.2.   Types of Religion Represented by Participants

Demographic Characteristic	Native N (%)	Judeo-Christian N (%)	Native American Church N (%)	Other N (%)	Unspecified N (%)
Gender (N=480)					
Male	90 (41%)	28 (34%)	5 (36%)	4 (80%)	68 (42%)
Female	127 (58%)	54 (66%)	9 (64%)	1 (20%)	94 (58%)
Age (N=480)					
18-29	65 (30%)	20 (24%)	7 (50%)	3 (60%)	66 (41%)
30-49	77 (35%)	29 (35%)	4 (29%)	1 (20%)	59 (36%)
50+	75 (35%)	33 (40%)	3 (21%)	1 (20%)	37 (23%)
Marital Status (N=467)					
Married/In a Relationship	114 (54%)	49 (61%)	5 (36%)	1 (20%)	78 (50%)
Never Married/ Divorced/ Separated/Widowed	97 (46%)	31 (39%)	9 (64%)	4 (80%)	79 (50%)
Children (N=474)					
Yes	147 (69%)	57 (70%)	9 (64%)	1 (20%)	106 (67%)
No	67 (31%)	25 (30%)	5 (36%)	4 (80%)	53 (33%)

Demographic Characteristic	Native N (%)	Judeo-Christian N (%)	Native American Church N (%)	Other N (%)	Unspecified N (%)
Education Level (N=473)					
GED or High School	41 (19%)	9 (11%)	5 (36%)	1 (20%)	54 (34%)
Post-High School			7 (50%)		64 (40%)
Training or 2-year College Degree	86 (40%)	34 (42%)		2 (40%)	
4-year College Degree or Higher	86 (40%)	38 (47%)	2 (14%)	2 (40%)	42 (26%)
Employment Status (N=472)					
Currently Employed	150 (70%)	62 (76%)	8 (57%)	3 (60%)	109 (69%)
Not Currently Employed	63 (30%)	20 (24%)	6 (43%)	2 (40%)	49 (31%)
American Indian Alone or Mixed Race (N=480)					
American Indian	172 (79%)	60 (73%)	10 (71%)	4 (80%)	124 (77%)
American Indian in Combination with Another Race/ Ethnicity	45 (21%)	22 (27%)	4 (29%)	1 (20%)	38 (23%)
Enrollment Status (N=472)					
Enrolled	179 (84%)	73 (89%)	11 (79%)	4 (80%)	124 (79%)
Not Enrolled	35 (16%)	9 (11%)	3 (21%)	1 (20%)	33 (21%)
Area Where Raised (N=476)					
Reservation or Tribal Trust Land	116 (54%)	28 (34%)	8 (57%)	1 (20%)	86 (54%)
Off-Reservation	99 (46%)	54 (66%)	6 (43%)	4 (80%)	74 (46%)
Culture Area (N=510)					
California	18 (8%)	6 (7%)	2 (14%)	0 (0%)	10 (6%)
Great Basin & Plateau	21 (10%)	7 (9%)	1 (7%)	0 (0%)	10 (6%)
Great Lakes	38 (18%)	18 (22%)	4 (29%)	1 (20%)	21 (13%)
Northeast & Southeast	18 (8%)	8 (10%)	0 (0%)	1 (20%)	17 (10%)
Northern Plains	26 (12%)	9 (11%)	1 (7%)	3 (60%)	25 (15%)
Northwest Coast, Arctic, Subarctic	17 (8%)	10 (12%)	0 (0%)	0 (0%)	9 (6%)
Southern Plains	47 (22%)	17 (21%)	4 (29%)	0 (0%)	42 (26%)
Southwest	32 (15%)	7 (9%)	2 (14%)	0 (0%)	28 (17%)

NOTE: Total N for each demographic variable are different based on whether or not an individual answered the demographic question. Percentages are presented as column percentages. Percentages may not total 100 due to rounding.

Credit: Christine M. Daley, Charley Lewis, and Joseph Pacheco

Conclusion

Understanding American Indian religious and spiritual traditions has been a fascination of scholars, religious authorities, government officials, and the general public for much of the history of Indian and White interactions since the beginnings of colonialism in the Americas. Much of this passion has resulted in misunderstandings and misrepresentations of Indigenous religions and spiritualities as primitive and heathen (Deloria 1992; Looking Horse 2003). This confusion, supported by colonialist greed and governmental indifference, fueled efforts to irradicate or assimilate Indigenous peoples. Where this has not been the case, the inverse enchantment with these traditions has led to further misinterpretation, appropriation, and exploitation by non-Natives who seek spiritual connection (Aldred 2000). These factors, alongside harmful stereotypes that suggest all Native peoples are overly spiritual and practice Indigenous spiritual traditions, have stymied scholarly and public understandings of Indigenous religious and spiritual practices.

Although a significant variation is present among Native peoples and their communities, an attempt has been made here to paint a general picture of religion and spirituality across Native North America based on *Native 24/7* participants. This broad overview is useful for a number of reasons. First, it subverts prevailing ideas about the assumed overly spiritual and sacred nature of American Indian existence. While many people in the general public assume that Native peoples are inherently spiritual and connected to their environments, influenced partly by popular depictions of Indigenous peoples such as the infamous Iron Eyes Cody "Crying Indian" commercials, *Native 24/7* findings suggest that, like other groups in the United States, the influence of historical circumstances, life experiences, and family relationships strongly determine how an individual does or does not align with a particular religious or spiritual tradition (Pearce and Thornton 2007; Peek 2005). *Native 24/7* participants revealed that practice and belief in Christian teachings, or any other religions for that matter, were not seen as problematic or making an individual any less "Native" in the eyes of a majority of their peers.

Second, these findings are useful for researchers seeking to work with heterogeneous American Indian communities or across multiple communities. Increasingly, American Indian peoples do not live on reservations or on tribal lands, but in urban communities. These communities are made up of a wide array of peoples that represent a collection of Native religious and spiritual traditions, alongside other traditions they may practice. This presents difficulties in the cultural tailoring process when attempting to design programming or materials that are relevant and respectful of beliefs from a variety of cultural and spiritual traditions. The findings here can provide some elemental considerations when dealing with Native religious and spiritual practice in these contexts.

Ultimately, *Native 24/7* participants have revealed that religious and spiritual practices remain a marker of identity among American Indians regardless of the traditions practiced. While the history of Native religions and spiritualities since the arrival of Europeans has been plagued by countless attempts to erase, exploit, or romanticize these traditions, conversations with participants not only reveal that these traditions have remained, but are not static nor locked in a particular point in time that denies Native agency and adaptation. To the contrary, the picture revealed by these discussions shows that, in many communities, spiritual traditions, religions, and multiple religious belongings remain strong. While being rooted in historical practice and belief, Native religious and spiritual practice is not confined to simplistic understandings of Pre-Contact traditions. Rather, American Indian community members' religious and spiritual practices represent traditions that have continued to adapt and change to ever-evolving circumstances, evidencing their openness and pluralistic understanding of religion and spirituality.

Notes

1. 22-year-old female from a Southwest rural community.
2. 40-year-old male from a Northern Plains reservation community.
3. 30-year-old male participant from a Plateau reservation community.
4. 23-year-old female from a Northern Plains reservation community.
5. 70-year-old female from a Southern Plains urban community.
6. 67-year-old male from a Plateau urban community.
7. 29-year-old male from a Northern Plains rural community.
8. 24-year-old female from a Great Basin rural community.
9. 67-year-old male from a Plateau urban community, 29-year-old male from a Northern Plains rural community, and 48-year-old male from Northern Plains rural community.
10. 23-year-old female from a Northern Plains reservation community and 50-year-old female from a Northern Plains reservation community.
11. 50-year-old female from a Northern Plains reservation community.
12. 26-year-old female from a California reservation community.
13. 24-year-old male from a Southwest urban community.
14. 56-year-old female from a Southwest reservation community.
15. 30-year-old female from a Great Lakes urban community.
16. 26-year-old female from a California reservation community.
17. 24-year-old male from a Plateau rural community.

18. 76-year-old female from a Great Lakes reservation community.
19. 19-year-old female from a Plateau rural community.
20. 27-year-old female from a Great Basin urban community.
21. 25-year-old male from a Southwest reservation community.
22. 18-year-old female from a Great Basin urban community.
23. 21-year-old female from a Southwest reservation community.
24. 74-year-old female from a Great Lakes reservation community.
25. 24-year-old female a Great Basin rural community.
26. 24-year-old male from a Southwest urban community.
27. 63-year-old female from a Great Lakes urban community.
28. 53-year-old male from a California reservation community.
29. 37-year-old male from a Northern Plains reservation community.
30. 64-year-old female from a Great Lakes urban community.
31. 54-year-old female from a California urban community.
32. 28-year-old female from a Great Lakes reservation community.
33. 43-year-old female from a Plateau rural community.
34. 54-year-old female from a Great Lakes urban community.
35. 58-year-old male from a Southern Plains rural community.

CHAPTER SIX

~

"A Necessary Evil"

Certificate of Degree of Indian Blood Cards

"Tunkaśila, he made me an Indian, not a piece of paper."

Mr. Harold Frazier, chairman of the Cheyenne River Sioux Tribe
Reclamation of Independence Declaration, July 4, 2017

There are currently about 1.9 million individuals enrolled in the 574 federally recognized American Indian nations and Alaska Native villages/corporations in the United States (BIA 2021). However, who gets to call himself or herself an American Indian or an Alaska Native today in the United States is not a simple matter, and in some respects, it has not been simple since Natives and non-Natives began regularly dealing with one another over five hundred years ago. Determining who is and who is not Native, specifically for tribal and US federal governmental purposes, has historical roots dating back to the early 1800s. "As the US government dispossessed Native peoples, treaties established specific rights, privileges, goods, and money to which those party to a treaty—both tribes as entities and individual tribal members—were entitled. The practices of creating formal censuses and keeping lists of names of tribal members evolved to ensure an accurate and equitable distribution of benefits" (Thornton 1996, 5).

According to the Bureau of Indian Affairs (BIA), one of the US federal governmental agencies tasked with dealing with Indian matters:

As a general rule, an American Indian or Alaska Native person is someone who has a blood degree from and is recognized as such by a federally recognized tribe or village (as an enrolled tribal member) and/or the United States. Of course, blood quantum (the degree of American Indian or Alaska Native blood from a federally recognized tribe or village that a person possesses) is not the only means by which a person is considered to be an American Indian or Alaska Native. Other factors, such as a person's knowledge of his or her tribe's culture, history, language, religion, familial kinships, and how strongly a person identifies himself or herself as American Indian or Alaska Native, are also important. In fact, there is no single federal or tribal criterion or standard that establishes a person's identity as American Indian or Alaska Native (2017a, 2017b, and 2017c).

While the above statement may be true in an "academic" sense, it does not always translate to everyday life as American Indians themselves often employ definitions different from that of the US federal government as to who is and who is not Indian, as well as what criteria are used to determine one's status as an Indian. According to Thornton (2005):

Many separate criteria may be used to delimit the Native American population. Language, residence, cultural affiliation, recognition by a community, degree of "blood," genealogical lines of descent, and self-identification have all been used at some point in the past to define both the total Native American population and specific tribal populations. Each measure produces a different population. Which variables are ultimately employed to define a population is an arbitrary decision; however, the implications for Native Americans can be enormous (28–29).

Adding to the complexity of all of this is the fact that American Indians and Alaska Natives are technically not a racial or ethnic group[1] *per se* in the eyes of the US federal government, but rather a political group due to the US federal government's unique political relationship with Indian nations (Balu 1995, 10). The treaties signed between the US federal government and Indian nations were signed between *sovereign nations*, and as such, race and ethnicity are secondary here to the sovereign status of Indian nations. This idea was reinforced in the 1974 Supreme Court case *Morton v. Mancari*. For some time, the BIA reiterated this on its website as well, where it stated:

The rights, protections, and services provided by the United States to individual American Indians and Alaska Natives flow not from a person's identity as such in an ethnological sense, but because he or she is a member of a federally recognized tribe. That is, a tribe that has a *government-to-government relationship* and a *special trust relationship* with the United States. These special trust and government-to-government relationships entail certain legally enforceable obligations and responsibilities on the part of the United States to persons who are enrolled members of such tribes (2017b, emphasis added).

Blood Quantum and Lineal Descent

Currently, there are two ways in which "Indianness" is determined—blood quantum and lineal descent. Blood quantum is essentially the percentage of Indian "blood" an individual possesses, such as full, one-half, one-quarter, etc. With lineal descent, there is no minimum blood quantum; however, an individual must have a verifiable ancestor who was Native and is on a tribe's official rolls. Presently, Indian tribes use both; the US federal government uses and prefers blood quantum but will accept lineal descent if that is what the tribe chooses.

In 1871, the United States federal government ended treaty making with Indian nations and moved to using Executive Orders and Congressional Acts to "deal with" Native peoples; this was largely due to the fact that sovereignty and self-determination were no longer seen as important as Native peoples were to be assimilated into the larger American society. However, the US federal government had used language referring to Indian blood going back to the early 1800s. As noted by Schmidt (2011), "One of the earliest references to treaties with language of 'half-bloods,' 'half-breeds,' or 'quarter-bloods' [was] in 1817 to grant various benefits usually land and money, to mixed individuals" (Schmidt 2011). Despite this precedent, it was not until the later decades of the nineteenth century when Indian blood and blood quantum started to become important designations of "Indianness" for the federal government (Spruhan 2006).

To "encourage" Native peoples to assimilate into American society, Congress passed the General Allotment Act, also known as the Dawes Severalty Act, of 1887. The purpose of this act was to divide up tribal lands and give allotments, or 160-acre or 80-acre parcels of what was once tribal land, to individual Native people to encourage mainstream agricultural endeavors and private land ownership. The criterion used to determine allotment eligibility was an individual's Indian blood quantum. According to Pewewardy (2003):

Determining blood quantum, however, required a benchmark, so beginning shortly after the passage of the act, federal enumerators began canvassing tribal lands, counting tribal households, and recording the number of adults and children and the blood quantum of each. Given that few Indigenous People possessed "official" birth certificates, enumerators had to rely on subjective judgment, individual self-report, and information supplied by neighbors, friends, and relatives. Compiled into what became known as the Dawes rolls, these records continue to be used for tribal enrollment decisions and determination of eligibility for special programs and services provided by the federal government for Indigenous People (78).

Currently, Indian nations have varying degrees of blood quantum required to be a member of a given nation or tribe. There is no DNA or blood testing done to determine blood quantum; rather, each nation chooses a specific tribal roll from a particular date from which they will determine an individual's blood quantum. Individuals whose names appear on the tribal roll on which blood quantum is based are considered to be 100 percent Native, from that specific tribe, unless documented differently on that roll. Prior intermarriage to other Natives or non-Natives does not impact the blood quantum of the individual on the roll. Therefore, this is a somewhat arbitrary designation of blood quantum and should not be considered a biological measure of DNA or "Indianness" for the purposes of academic discussion or genetic study. Each tribe selects the time period from which it will determine blood quantum based on tribal history, availability of records, or other tribe-specific details. These decisions are appropriate from a cultural standpoint.

For example, the Navajo Nation requires members to have at least a 25 percent Navajo blood quantum based on an ancestor listed on the January 1940 Navajo Tribal Roll. The White Mountain Apache Tribe requires that all members have at least a 50 percent overall Indian blood quantum, and that 25 percent of that blood quantum must be White Mountain Apache. Like the Navajo, the White Mountain Apache maintain a tribal membership roll. Anyone applying for membership must have a direct lineal descendant or descendants on the membership roll. The Bureau of Indian Affairs requires a person to have at least a 25 percent Indian blood quantum to apply for a Certificate of Degree of Indian Blood (CDIB) card. A CDIB card is an official US federal government document detailing an individual's tribal affiliation and blood quantum. This card is what is often used by a Native individual who is seeking to access federal governmental services reserved for Indian peoples. These services are most often reserved for Indian peoples because of treaties and legal agreements.

In 1934, Congress passed the Indian Reorganization Act (IRA), also known as the Wheeler-Howard Act or Public Law 73-383. It was part of what is called the "Indian New Deal" which aimed to decrease US federal government control in Indian matters and allow for increased self-determination. The pros and cons of the Indian New Deal and IRA are still debated today, but regardless, one of the provisions of IRA called for tribes to adopt written constitutions. Many tribes have provisions within their constitutions that address tribal membership, both historically and presently. Because of this, a tribe has the right to decide whether to use blood quantum or lineal descent to determine membership. With lineal descent, a person must have a verifiable ancestor who was a tribal member, however, there is no minimum blood quantum. As long as an individual has an ancestor on a tribal roll, he or she is eligible to be a tribal member. For example, the Osage Nation requires an individual seeking enrollment to have a lineal ancestor listed on the Osage Allotment Act of 1906. The degree or percentage of that relationship is irrelevant; one just needs to have a lineal ancestor on the roll.

Both blood quantum and lineal descent have pros and cons. Blood quantum is often criticized as being too exclusive, while lineal descent is often criticized as being too inclusive. As noted by Fletcher (2012–2013), "Blood quantum rules create strange, if not downright untenable, outcomes. . . . Lineal descendancy, however, also generates strange outcomes relating to tribal identity. . . . Lineal descendancy casts a much wider net to include tribal members, but it may also be dramatically over inclusive" (6).

Tribal Enrollment Cards and Certificate of Degree of Indian Blood Cards

Regardless, "tribal enrollment requirements preserve the unique character and traditions of each tribe. The tribe establishes membership criteria based on shared customs, traditions, language and tribal blood. . . . Tribal enrollment criteria are set forth in tribal constitutions, articles of incorporation or ordinances. The criterion varies from tribe to tribe, so uniform membership requirements do not exist" (Bureau of Indian Affairs 2019). Tribal enrollment, as well as the accompanying tribal enrollment card, is generally required to access tribal services and programs on reservations, specifically those sponsored and funded by the tribe itself. For example, some reservation-based communities have both an Indian Health Services clinic and a tribally run health clinic, also known as a 638-clinic, referencing the Indian Self-Determination and Education Assistance Act of 1975 (Public Law 93-638), which, among other things, allowed tribes to set up contracts with the federal government to administratively control various resources, including health care facilities. Any American Indian residing on that reservation and in possession of a CDIB or tribal enrollment card can use the IHS clinic; however, in some cases only those enrolled in that tribe can use the 638-clinic.

Individuals who meet the US federal government's required blood quantum criterion (25%) are eligible to apply for a Certificate of Degree of Indian

Blood (CDIB) card. A CDIB card, provided by the US federal government's Bureau of Indian Affairs, allows individuals who have documented Native ancestry and are descended from one of the federally recognized American Indian and Alaska Native nations to access governmental services and programs designated solely for Native peoples. While CDIB cards are in theory beneficial to Native peoples, as they are needed to access governmental services and programs, such as Indian Health Services and Bureau of Indian Education programs, they are also surrounded by controversy and considered very problematic by many Native people. Many Indians view CDIB cards as an extension of the American colonial system because no other racial or ethnic group in the US has a similar governmental card. Some Natives, however, see CDIB cards as a way for Indian people to keep the services and programs designated for them through treaties, executive orders, acts of Congress, and US federal court decisions out of the hands of non-Natives and people with questionable Indian ancestry.

There is, however, a difference between a CDIB card and a tribal enrollment card. Just because an individual has a CDIB card does not mean that he or she is enrolled in a tribe. Because a CDIB card is issued by the Bureau of Indian Affairs, the person who holds the card just needs to meet the BIA's one-quarter Indian blood quantum. If that individual can show, on paper via birth certificates, death certificates, etc., a connection to a biological family member who was a member of a tribe, and that the individual can meet the one-quarter blood quantum, the BIA will issue that petitioning individual a CDIB card that shows his/her blood quantum and *tribal affiliation* (Bureau of Indian Affairs 2019). What is important here is the wording—tribal affiliation—as this does not imply enrollment or membership in a tribe, rather just an affiliation or connection. However, because tribes themselves determine tribal membership, the requirements for tribal membership do not have to follow the same rules as a CDIB. The blood quantum could be higher or lower; there may be a residency requirement; the connection may be required to be through the maternal or paternal line; and so forth. Likewise, a person can have a tribal enrollment card but not a CDIB card. Many Native people have tribal enrollment cards but not CDIB cards because most of the time a tribal enrollment card will be more beneficial in terms of accessing tribal and US federal governmental programs than a CDIB card.

There are some cases in which a tribal enrollment card is less beneficial; this is when the tribal enrollment card comes from a state recognized tribe. Because state recognized tribes are not recognized by the US federal government, they cannot be used to access any federal governmental programs.

State recognized tribal enrollment cards generally only allow for access to services and programs in the state in which the state recognized tribe resides.

Under the Indian Self-Determination and Education Assistance Act of 1975 (P.L. 93-638), federally recognized tribes, but not state recognized, have the right to contract with US federal government agencies to provide services to themselves instead of having the services administered through US federal agencies. Services connected to health care, education, and welfare are most commonly contracted, and this often includes issuing CDIB cards. "A CDIB may be issued directly by the BIA or by a tribal government operating under a '638' contract, but with no clear rules to govern how those offices grant or deny CDIB or calculate the blood quantum listed on the document" (Krol 2018). Because of this, obtaining CDIB and tribal enrollment cards can get complicated and, in some cases, can be very difficult.

David Cornsilk (2008), a professional genealogist and enrolled member of the Cherokee Nation of Oklahoma, documents the history of CDIB cards and tribal enrollment cards among the Cherokee Nation of Oklahoma:

> The BIA began, as early as 1920 (perhaps even earlier), issuing a letter to (Cherokee) enrollees on the Dawes Roll called a Certificate of Enrollment. This document was also issued to their descendants and showed the name of the enrollee, his/her tribe and blood quantum if any. . . . Around 1946, the BIA began issuing a Certificate of Indian Descent or CID. The documents, on 8 × 11 paper . . . were given to the living enrollee and showed his/her blood quantum as found on the Dawes Roll or, if the enrollee was dead, CID was issued to the lineal heirs showing their blood quantum as computed from the ancestor. . . . The CID was issued to individuals without them being asked for much documentation. Many erroneous CIDs were issued. It was the philosophy of the BIA, right up to 1984 when tribes began contracting the CDIB program, that only an Indian would claim to be Indian. Obviously, they were wrong. . . . Around 1970 . . . the BIA began issuing what was called a Certificate of Degree of Indian Blood or CDIB. It too was a piece of paper carried by the individual showing lineal descent from a Dawes enrollee with a degree of blood and the degree of blood computed for the individual from the ancestor(s). . . . Sometime around 1977, the BIA began issuing what they called a Certificate of Degree of Indian Blood card. The process for obtaining a CDIB remained the same, but the paper document stayed with the BIA and a facsimile was issued to the applicant, along with a small card showing the name of the individual, his tribe, blood quantum, date of birth and signature of the issuing officer. . . . In 1984 . . . the Cherokee Nation contracted the CDIB Card program from the BIA. Since that time, CDIB cards for Cherokee have been issued by the Cherokee Nation Registration Office. However, the CDIB still had to show approval by an officer employed by the BIA with his/her signature. . . . I'm not

sure how long ago this happened, but the BIA has relinquished to the tribes the full authority to issue the CDIB and cards, thus only requiring the signature of the authorized tribal officia. (Cornsilk 2008)

Native 24/7 Participant Views on CDIB Cards

In his 1969 seminal work, *Custer Died for Your Sins*, Lakota scholar Vine Deloria Jr. stated, "Into each life, it is said, some rain must fall. Some people have bad horoscopes, others take tips on the stock market. McNamara created the TFX and the Edsel. Churches possess the real world. But Indians have been cursed above all other people in history. Indians have anthropologists" (Deloria 1969, 78). If Deloria wrote this today, it is possible that CDIB cards would be added to his list.

Native 24/7 sought to examine the CDIB card phenomenon, specifically peoples' thoughts and feelings about the card. It has been our experience that CDIB cards can be controversial and divisive, as well as confusing and elusive. We have all met someone who talks about getting the paperwork in order so he/she can get his/her "Indian card." On the *Native 24/7* demographic survey, participants were asked their tribal affiliation(s) and if they were enrolled in a tribe. They were also asked a question during the open-ended interviews about CDIB cards, specifically seeking thoughts and feelings on the cards. We did not, however, ask questions about tribal enrollment cards, though they came up often in our discussions about CDIB cards.

Of the 734 participants in *Native 24/7*, 636 completed some or all of the survey questions, which included their tribal affiliation and enrollment status. All but 16 individuals answered the question of whether or not they were enrolled in a tribe, and 508 provided a tribal affiliation. Of those who answered the question about enrollment, 82 percent (509 individuals) claimed to be enrolled in a tribe. These individuals represented 121 unique tribal affiliations, with 87 naming multiple tribal affiliations. Five did not provide a tribal affiliation. Of those who were not enrolled in a tribe, four did not provide a tribal affiliation at all, 85 provided one affiliation, and 22 provided more than one. Sixty-three unique tribal affiliations were represented among the individuals who were not enrolled in a tribe.

As previously discussed, 612 individuals completed the interview portion of the study and were asked the open question about their thoughts on CDIB cards; 609 responded to that question. To allow for comparison across survey and interview data, we coded the textual data from the interviews for statistical analyses (described in the introductory chapter). For the question regarding CDIB cards, we categorized interview responses regarding participants' overall feelings concerning CDIB cards as positive, negative, neutral/

ambivalent, and did not know what a CDIB card is (see figure 6.1 and table 6.1). Most participants (37%) were neutral or ambivalent when it came to CDIB cards, seeing them as a double-edged sword or, as the subtitle of this chapter suggests, a necessary evil. The idea that CDIB cards are a "necessary evil" comes from this very straightforward and simple response to describing CDIB cards from a forty-nine-year-old female study participant from the Southern Plains. After neutral or ambivalent feelings toward CDIBs, similar portions of participants viewed them as negative (24%) or positive (24%). A very small portion of participants were unsure what a CDIB card is (4%).

Views on CDIB cards were examined by demographic variables, similar to other influences. Participant views on CDIB cards were influenced by these factors in different ways, with some factors more important than others. Gender was not an important factor in influencing view, though men were slightly more likely to have a negative view of CDIB cards. Reasons for this negative viewpoint appeared to focus on the fact that CDIB cards are not a true measure of ties to culture and traditionality, with many of them saying that CDIB cards are not traditional and almost half saying that they are a tool of the government harkening back to Termination policies. They expressed a need for measures of culture or traditionality rather than lineage or blood quantum.

Age had more influence on views on CDIB cards, with a trend toward a more positive view among older individuals (over age 50) and trend toward

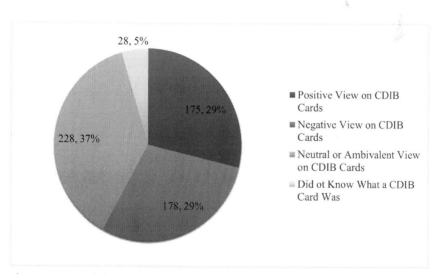

Figure 6.1. Participant Views on CDIB Cards by Demographic Variables (N=609).
Credit: Christine M. Daley, Charley Lewis, and Joseph Pacheco.

Table 6.1. Participant Views on CDIB Cards by Demographic Variables

Demographic Characteristic	Positive View on CDIB Cards N (%)	Negative View on CDIB Cards N (%)	Neutral or Ambivalent View on CDIB Cards N (%)	Did Not Know What a CDIB Card Is N (%)
Gender (N=609)				
Male	67 (38%)	76 (43%)	83 (36%)	10 (36%)
Female	108 (62%)	102 (57%)	145 (64%)	18 (64%)
Age (N=613)				
18-29	55 (31%)	59 (33%)	80 (34%)	19 (68%)
30-49	57 (33%)	68 (38%)	98 (42%)	4 (14%)
50+	63 (36%)	51 (29%)	54 (23%)	5 (18%)
Marital Status				
Married/In a Relationship	77 (56%)	86 (57%)	96 (49%)	7 (33%)
Never Married/Divorced/Separated/ Widowed	61 (44%)	64 (43%)	98 (51%)	14 (67%)
Children (N=514)				
Yes	101 (71%)	111 (72%)	126 (65%)	9 (41%)
No	42 (29%)	43 (28%)	69 (35%)	13 (59%)
Education Level (N=514)				
GED or High School	59 (41%)	23 (15%)	51 (26%)	11 (50%)
Post-High School Training or 2-year College Degree	55 (38%)	75 (49%)	76 (39%)	9 (41%)
4-year College Degree or Higher	30 (21%)	55 (36%)	68 (35%)	2 (9%)
Employment Status				
Currently Employed	93 (65%)	105 (70%)	145 (74%)	14 (64%)
Not Currently Employed	50 (35%)	45 (30%)	50 (26%)	8 (36%)
American Indian Alone or Mixed Race (N=520)				
American Indian	122 (85%)	113 (73%)	158 (79%)	15 (68%)
American Indian in Combination with Another Race/Ethnicity	22 (15%)	42 (27%)	41 (21%)	7 (32%)
Enrollment Status (N=510)				
Enrolled	117 (84%)	125 (82%)	165 (83%)	16 (76%)
Not Enrolled	22 (16%)	27 (18%)	33 (17%)	5 (24%)
Area Where Raised (N=516)				
Reservation or Tribal Trust Land	79 (55%)	86 (56%)	104 (53%)	10 (45%)
Off-Reservation	64 (45%)	68 (44%)	93 (47%)	12 (55%)
Culture Area (N=609)				
California	15 (9%)	13 (7%)	15 (7%)	5 (18%)
Great Basin & Plateau	19 (11%)	12 (7%)	20 (9%)	4 (14%)
Great Lakes	29 (17%)	34 (19%)	28 (12%)	7 (25%)
Northeast & Southeast	17 (10%)	21 (12%)	19 (8%)	2 (7%)
Northern Plains	24 (14%)	33 (19%)	52 (23%)	6 (21%)
Northwest Coast, Arctic, Subarctic	9 (5%)	9 (5%)	16 (7%)	0 (0%)
Southern Plains	28 (16%)	37 (21%)	52 (23%)	0 (0%)
Southwest	34 (19%)	19 (11%)	26 (11%)	4 (14%)

NOTE: Total N for each demographic variable are different based on whether or not an individual answered the demographic question. Percentages are presented as column percentages. Percentages may not total 100 due to rounding.

Credit: Christine M. Daley, Charley Lewis, and Joseph Pacheco

a more neutral or ambivalent view among those under age 50, particularly among those age 18–29. Individuals between ages 30 and 49 had neutral or ambivalent views trending toward negative views. Among elders, the dominant view was that these cards should imbue the individual with a sense of pride for who they are, though there was also a consensus that the system of blood quantum is flawed and should be changed. This may be because people in this age group have had a longer history of dealing with US federal governmental policies and procedures and have come to view the CDIB card differently because of this. Additionally, participants in this age group are more likely to have either attended boarding schools themselves or had a mother, father, or close family member who attended boarding school. Their perspectives on CDIB cards were likely influenced by experiences with boarding schools in a way that younger generations were not.

For those in their thirties and forties, feelings on CDIB cards were driven by how the cards affected their children and access to services. Those in their twenties focused on problems with how the cards are attained, particularly problems with blood quantum. This age group was also the most likely to not know what a CDIB card is. It is likely that the younger generation would be more likely to have trouble getting a CDIB card because of blood quantum rules. Over time, intermarriage has become more common among different tribes and between Natives and non-Natives, thus causing problems for children meeting certain blood quantum rules. It is likely that these problems influenced the views of participants in this age group.

Individuals who were married were somewhat more likely to have stronger feelings about the cards and were less likely to not know what they are. These trends are likely tied to participant ages and whether or not they had children. Driven by the center age group (30–49), individuals with children were more likely to have a strong viewpoint on CDIB cards rather than being neutral or ambivalent. The driving factor behind ambivalence was access to services, tied to their children's ability to access services based on whether or not they could be enrolled. Participants with children were more likely to talk about the need to tie obtainment of CDIB cards to tradition and culture.

Formal education level appears to have an interesting impact on views of CDIB cards, with participants with some post-high school education, but no bachelor's degree, having the most negative view. Those with less formal education have the most positive views, and those with the highest levels of formal education had the most ambivalent views, recognizing both positive and negative aspects of CDIB cards. It would appear that formal education initially has the effect of lowering an individual's view of CDIB cards, but over additional formal education that view is tempered. Those with lower educational attainment focused on pride and access to services as a reason for their positive views. Those in the middle education group primarily cited problems with blood quantum and the cards as a tool of Termination or the government as reasons for their views. The highest educated group provided many reasons for their ambivalent views, including those represented by both other groups, though only one-third of them talked about blood quantum itself. Rather, in terms of negative views, this group focused on the need for additional criteria and more ties to culture and tradition (nearly two-thirds) and the fact that the cards can easily be seen as a tool of the government tied to Termination policies (over 50%). Nearly half also focused on the use of CDIB cards to keep others out of their communities and allow access to services only to those in their communities as a positive aspect. Thus, initially, higher education causes many Native people to recognize the problems associated with CDIB cards, but ultimately provides a more complex understanding of both their positive and negative aspects.

Employment status did not appear to have a strong influence on views of CDIB cards. People who were currently employed showed somewhat of a tendency toward neutral, ambivalent, or negative views. Those who were unemployed tended toward having either positive or negative views rather than ambivalent or neutral. Reasons tied to employment were not much discussed; it is, therefore, likely the viewpoints within these groups of employed versus not employed are driven by other factors.

Individuals who claimed only Native heritage were more likely to have positive or ambivalent views on CDIB cards; those with mixed heritage tended to have more negative views. People who claimed only Native heritage focused on discussions of Native pride and keeping others out of their communities or accessing services meant for their communities. They also spoke about problems with blood quantum and were more likely than others to feel the blood quantum should be raised. Those with mixed heritage explained their feelings through a need for ties to culture and tradition to be more important for obtaining a CDIB card and a focus on cards as a tool of Termination. It is likely that these views are also influenced by changing marriage and child-bearing customs.

Enrollment status had little effect on feelings about CDIB cards. Those who were not enrolled were somewhat more likely to know what CDIB cards are, though some enrolled members of tribes still claimed no knowledge of them. Positive versus negative views were similar among those who were enrolled and those who were not.

Being raised on a reservation was not an important determinant in terms of the view of CDIB card; however, the part of the country in which an individual was raised had some influence. Individuals raised in both the Northern and Southern Plains were more likely to have negative views of CDIB cards, while those in the Southwest tended to have more positive views. Those from California, the Great Basin and Plateau, the Great Lakes, and the Northeast and Southeast were less likely to be neutral or ambivalent in their feelings, but were not clearly more negative or positive in their views. The small sample from the Northwest Coast, Arctic, and Subarctic did not show any clear trends in their views. People from the Southern Plains were more likely than others to talk about services as a determining reason for their views. People from the Northern Plains were more likely to talk about problems with the way blood quantum is determined as their primary reason for their views. No other clear trends by region of the country were determined for reasons for their views.

One factor that may impact the influence of where an individual grew up is the residential fluidity that is common among many American Indian peoples. Many participants were raised in multiple environments even though they primarily associate with one; this is common for many Native people. Often an individual will spend part of the year on a reservation in his or her home community and then part of the same year in a rural or urban community because of seasonal employment or temporary job opportunities, only to return to their reservation home community when that job ends. Individuals will continue doing this as jobs and employment opportunities present themselves. Often children will accompany parents during these treks back and forth to and from the reservation, or rural areas. In addition, Native individuals who have moved away from the reservation for educational reasons or for employment and are now living in urban environments still refer to themselves as reservation Indians because that is where they were raised, even though they no longer live on a reservation and have no plans to return there any time in the near future.

Reasons for Beliefs about CDIB Cards

When the reasons participants gave as to why they viewed CDIB cards the way they did are viewed as a whole, they divide into fifteen categories. These reasons are shown in figure 6.2.

Overall, thoughts and feelings on CDIB cards were mixed; some participants thought CDIB cards were useful and needed, while others did not. Even among those who felt CDIB cards were either positive or negative, there were different reasons as to why they were positive or negative. Positive feelings concerning CDIB cards were mostly linked to tribal enrollment and accessing tribal and federal governmental services. The same is true for those

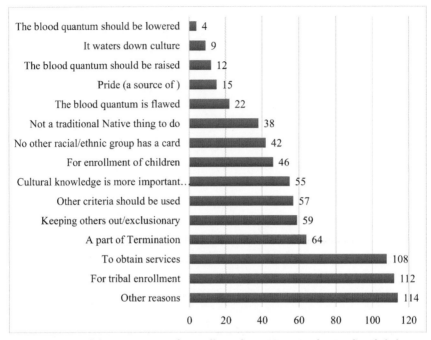

Figure 6.2. Participants' Reasons for Feelings about CDIB Cards. *Credit*: Christine M. Daley, Charley Lewis, and Joseph Pacheco.

who thought they were negative. Negative feelings were mainly connected to CDIB cards being viewed as an extension of US federal government Termination programs and policies, not being a Native way to do things, and the fact that no other racial or ethnic group is required to carry documentation as proof of identity. Additionally, many participants viewed CDIB cards in an ambivalent or neutral light, as if they were a "double-edged sword." Some things about CDIB cards are good, others are not. When the interview data are examined closely, nuanced thoughts and feelings emerge beyond the information found in the quantitative data.

According to cultural anthropologist, Robert Bee (1999), there are three attributes of a colonial situation: (1) economic exploitation, (2) political domination, and (3) cultural domination. In economic exploitation, the local peoples are exploited as slaves or a cheap labor source, and their natural resources and lands are exploited as well. In political domination, local peoples no longer have their ability to govern themselves, rather they are subjugated to the laws, policies, and dictates of the colonizer. With cultural domination, the colonizer seeks to replace local beliefs, practices, and ways of life with those of its own so that the local people are assimilated and begin to follow the ways of the colonizer. Daley and Daley (2003), add a fourth attribute: medical domination. With medical domination, local peoples lose access to lands and resources, thus affecting their abilities to continue traditional healing practices. Additionally, loss of traditional forms of religion and spirituality further affects healing traditions as medicine, religion, and spirituality are linked in most cultures. Moreover, diseases introduced by the colonizer, either accidentally or purposely, take their tolls. In the end, the healing system of the colonizer usually becomes the dominant healing system, thus making medicine an extension of the colonial system.

American history is filled with examples of colonialism, ethnocide, and genocide aimed at American Indian peoples and their communities, including forced removal from ancestral homelands; the banning of cultural, religious, spiritual, and linguistic traditions; compulsory attendance at boarding schools, the forced sterilization of Native women; and many more examples. Of more recent history are the Termination Era programs of the 1950s–1970s, the current battles over oil pipelines, and the high numbers of missing and murdered Native women and girls. Colonization has greatly affected contemporary Native peoples, and it is important to remember that colonization in America is still occurring; it is not a thing of the past as many individuals perceive. Many *Native 24/7* participants pointed to CDIB cards as an example of modern-day colonialism. A Native woman from California explained:

> I think it is BS. I think CDIBs are BS. . . . We are the only racial group in the United States that has to prove who we are by blood. . . . The blood quantum was actually set up by the Federal government to prove who could and who couldn't be in charge of their assets. So, when it was first implemented, I believe it was if you were between a quarter and a full blood, you couldn't be in charge of your assets because according to the Federal government, you didn't have the skills to do that. So, they would give you an agent to be in charge of your stuff, and then with the formation of tribes it became this thing. It was something the tribes adopted to decide who was and wasn't part of the tribe. . . . This method that was implemented by the Federal government was never used before there was an America. . . . I just think it's not a system that Native Americans ever used before the Federal government, and I don't think it's a wise system to utilize to prove who is and who isn't Native American.[2]

Another Native woman from California reiterated this idea when she stated, "I don't really believe it's a good way to figure out who's Indian and who's not. That's kind of my own feelings about it. I just think it's the government's way *they* define Indian. It's not how *we* define Indian."[3] Along this same line of thought, an elder stated,

I guess CDIB, the Federal Government, that was their way of identifying who's an Indian, and for services. Now it's used by many tribes. . . . That's basically what it's for. Now, does that make us Indian or not make us Indian? Again, even if I didn't have a CDIB or a tribal enrollment card, I would still lead this same life that I have and I would still have the same beliefs, the same life and community and family that I was born into and raised by, so there would be no changing who I am. And, so, again, who is an Indian? What's an Indian? CDIB, tribal enrollment card, that's what, some kind of official identity? And for services? But so far as being Native, I can operate as a Native person because that's what I was born into. . . . I am a certain clan of a certain tribe, and these are the values that we operate by. This makes you Indian.[4]

In her 1987 work, *The Legacy of Conquest: The Unbroken Past of the American West*, historian Patricia Limerick states, "Set the blood quantum at one-quarter, hold to it as a rigid definition of Indians, let intermarriage proceed as it had for centuries, and eventually Indians will be defined out of existence. When that happens, the federal government will be freed of its persistent 'Indian problem'" (Schmidt 2011, 6). It was suggested by many participants that the blood quantum and CDIB cards were a form of modern genocide aimed at Native peoples, echoing Limerick's sentiment. A participant from the Southeast stated,

I think CDIB cards is just another way of genocide. . . . They had put a number on us. . . . They are trying to get rid of . . . Indian people as a whole. That's why they gave us those. We are the only people that have to have a card that proves who we are, which is, you know, not right, but it still stands today. . . . I think, eventually, that number is going to dwindle down to where there is nothing left.[5]

Another participant went on to say that he thought CDIB cards were ridiculous:

I think that they are kind of ridiculous. They've been instilled into most Native communities. . . . They're kind of a necessary part of being Indian now, and I don't necessarily agree with that. But I think that most people that are Indian do have one. But a hundred years ago, they didn't really have those. A hundred and twenty years ago, I know they didn't have those. It was started as a way for the government to kind of determine who was Indian, basically. . . . And some tribes have bought into that and some tribes haven't. . . . You know, when the government came in and assigned quantums, it wasn't done very accurately. It was done on both ends to reduce the quantum as much as possible. The government eventually wanted you to no longer be Indian. . . . They're not really useful . . . they're just an arbitrary piece of paper because every tribe had its own original way of determining who was a member.[6]

The idea behind this is not to get rid of Native people through conflict and warfare but rather through a diminishing bloodline. According to a participant from the Southwest, Creator is not going to ask to see your CDIB when you cross over. She stated,

> I think it is a governmental way of eventually eliminating us as Native Americans. My tribe . . . you have to be half in order to be recognized. You can be a descendant at ¼. . . . which is ridiculous. . . . They don't get the same services as if they were ½ . . . I think that we are going to be eliminated as a people in one or two generations. I think as long as you have Native blood, you believe in the culture, you believe in what being a Native American is and your tribe that you are, I don't need someone to tell me that you are only ½ or only ¼ of your blood is Native. . . . When I die and I meet the Creator, he's not going to ask me for my CDIB. He's going to know that I participated in the culture, that I participated in the things that we usually do to prepare to go into the next world. . . . So I think it's worthless.[7]

Another participant echoed this when she said,

> We've all been really programmed to buy into who's more Indian than someone else, or who's more Native, or who's got more blood, or you know whatever. But in my opinion, the importance is how much you give back to your community, how . . . you preserve your culture, how much do you fight to make sure we preserve our sovereignty. How involved are you? That should be more important than a number on a card, and plus that was something that was totally implemented by the Federal government anyway, I think as a way to eventually eradicate us anyway because if we have kids and they are not with the same tribal member then our blood degree just dwindles down and down and down. And by kind of talking us into believing that someone's more Native or more deserving just because of a number that the Federal government came up with I think we are totally buying into another form of genocide.[8]

In their 2012 article, "Decolonization Is Not a Metaphor," Eve Tuck and K. Wayne Yang echoed the above idea. They explain,

> Native Americans are constructed to become fewer in number and less Native, but never exactly White, over time. . . . That is, Native American is a racialization that portrays contemporary Indigenous generations to be less authentic, less Indigenous than every prior generation in order to ultimately phase out Indigenous claims to land and usher in settler claims to property. This (is)

primarily done through blood quantum registries and policies, which were forced in Indigenous nations and communities and, in some cases, have overshadowed former ways of determining tribal membership (12).

Furthermore, numerous participants stated that the blood quantum concept was not a Native way of determining tribal membership. An elder from the Southern Plains stated,

> As far as blood quantum is concerned, that was not a construction of American Indian people, that was a construction that was imposed that had very political and economic purposes and outcomes. The arguments that occur amongst American Indian people about blood quantum, who's a real Indian and who's not a real Indian, I think are divisive; I think do harm, particularly when they are targeted to children. . . . I think it's family and stories and friends and community and that whole cultural support system that shapes how a child comes to view him or herself, and that sustains them through adulthood that matter, not this notion, and again it's a constructed notion, of blood quantum that is verified by certificates of degree of Indian blood. Who else in the world has to carry a card around that says how much they are of this or that?[9]

The notion that American Indians are the only racial or ethnic group that must carry a card or paperwork to prove their racial or ethnic affiliation was brought up by many participants as well. One participant noted,

> It's an interesting position because you don't see other races . . . being classified [by] what percentage they are. [A person of] another race could just say, oh, I identify with this race and no one really questions it. But with Native Americans, there is kind of this sense of like, well are you really Native American? Or what percentage are you? Being forced to quantify yourself is . . . kind of demeaning, I would say.[10]

Interestingly, three participants from the Great Lakes area linked blood quantums and CDIB cards with animal pedigrees. One participant was direct and blunt when she explained, "Personally, I think it's bullshit, I hope you can put that in there (the book). It's just a way for the government to weed us out so they don't have to abide by the treaties they signed with our people a long time ago. . . . It makes me look at it as how animals—like dogs, thoroughbreds, horses. I don't think we should have to go by blood quantums."[11]

Two other Great Lakes participants supported this notion. One participant from a reservation community stated, "Well, there (are) what, three things the US government quantifies by blood? There's, like, horses and dogs, and Natives. So, it's a little offensive to me."[12] A participant from a Great Lakes urban community stated, "I think it makes us like pedigreed animals, and I don't like it. . . . On one hand I get it, because it's a screener for people who aren't really Native American. . . . I understand how people feel about that. But for me, it's another governmental tool to separate us and divide us."[13]

Additionally, numerous participants stated that CDIB cards are often incorrect because the blood quantum listed on the card is wrong. A twenty-seven-year-old female participant said, "I don't know, it just seems sometimes they're not right, cause, like, my mom, one of her CDIB cards she had from like the '80s says she was half Prairie Band Potawatomi and a quarter Citizen Band, and then they did it again and said she was a quarter of each. Then with my aunts and uncles, some of theirs read different. . . . All of them had the same mom and dad, so they should all still be the same blood, which is kind of crazy."[14]

Another participant had a similar experience; she stated, "Actually, after my father passed away, I found two cards of his showing that he was a registered American Indian. One of them showed one amount of blood and percent, and the other said another fact. So, I don't know which one is true."[15]

Participants also made claims that blood quantums and CDIB cards are divisive and cause problems among Indian peoples. A participant from a Great Lakes urban community explained,

> We try to claim our own sovereignty, but then again, we'll try to use the government's own what I call teaspoon. So, we are our own people, but then we are going to use the measuring spoon they (the US government) gave us by saying, OK, this person is only a tenth, so they don't qualify as being Native. Well, who are we to sit there and say if this person is following their ways . . . I'm sorry, you're only ten percent, so you don't count? I don't think we should use a measuring spoon like that.[16]

A participant from a Southwestern reservation agreed with the above; she said,

> Those make me really sad. I feel like those are an external form of forcing us to break ourselves into little pieces, and I don't know who really anymore today can call themselves 100% . . . and it makes me nervous when people start playing the numbers game. . . . My mom was the first person in her family to marry an Anglo, so I have firsthand experience of being treated like a second-class citizen in both worlds, in both my tribe and the larger society. So, for me, I

wish we could get away from those numbers and have a more organic way of letting people sense and feel where they belong and who they are.[17]

A male participant from the Southwest went on to say, "I think it's another form of separation, because we're using blood quantum to determine how much Native you are. It encourages other Natives to . . . look down upon each other. It increases the feeling of separation among people."[18]

Additionally, Native 24/7 participants stated that even if an individual does have an adequate blood quantum, that does not mean that he or she is going to be an active member of his or her nation or tribe. One participant explained,

> As far as the CDIB and blood quantums and such, from my experience from working with many groups of people, blood quantum is not necessarily an indicator of how someone will be committed to their tribal nation, communities, or family. And unfortunately, those words have made it into some of how Native folks have talked about each other. But you know, we also got to remember that while this person may be 1/64 or something like that, that they have a family member who has a major Native side to them and that their ancestors and relatives have done work so that they can be here today. And so, when I work with folks, that's something I keep in mind. And, you know, tribal nations and Indian people have enough problems right now that we need to focus our discourse and studies, and legal efforts, to improve the lives of Indian folks everywhere.[19]

A Southern Plains participant echoed this when she stated, "I don't think they should matter at all. I think that it's not about what degree of blood a piece of paper says you have. I think what matters is how you identify culturally, and how you see yourself, and how your Native peers see you, accept you, and believe you to be part of their tribe or bigger culture."[20]

As previously noted, there were many participants who thought CDIB cards were positive and were useful. Much of the reasoning for this perspective involved access to funds and services reserved for Native people. One participant noted CDIB cards were good for college students. She said, "I think it's good . . . especially for being a student, it does help with financial stuff. Because there's so many scholarships out there that you have to qualify for, and it's good that our tribe and other tribes offer scholarships to Native Americans that do claim a certain degree of a tribe."[21] Another participant said something very similar when she explained, "It helps when you are trying to go to college because when you're trying to apply for scholarships, or go to different schools, it helps out a lot in getting scholarships and things like that."[22]

Some participants also saw CDIB cards as a way to prove Native ancestry and as a source of Native pride. A participant from the Southwest said, "I think it's a good thing. I mean its proof to say you're part Native. Everything in this world has to be written down on paper to prove anything. You can't just be saying . . . I'm Native . . . there has to be some documentation to say you are Native. Anybody can say they're Native. . . . It's a good thing because it separates us from non-Native people."[23] This sentiment was echoed by a nineteen-year-old participant when she said, "I feel it's a must have for identification. Not so many Native Americans are around, and anyone could claim that they're . . . Native America. . . . This card tells you still the degree of how much you are Native American."[24]

Adding to this was the belief held by many participants that blood quantum and CDIB cards were needed to make sure non-Natives were not accessing services reserved specifically for Native peoples. An elder from the Northern Plains reservation stated, "Well, in this day and age, I unfortunately think it's necessary because . . . now that they think they can get something, everyone wants to be Indian."[25] Another participant reiterated this when she said, "I think it is a good thing, that we have cards, because if we didn't, we're going to have every Tom, Dick, and Harry trying to enroll in our tribes and take our benefits."[26]

An interesting point of comparison between positive and negative views of CDIB cards was that those who viewed CDIB cards negatively had more to say about them than those who viewed them positively. As previously illustrated, those who found them problematic had long and complex reasons as to why they were problematic. Those who did not find them problematic were very brief and basically said that they were good for accessing services, particularly scholarships, and showing someone that you were in fact Indian. There were no long or detailed justifications. However, those who were ambivalent or were neutral on the matter were more verbose and explanatory in their answers; more similar to those who had a negative stance on them.

Most *Native 24/7* participants (36.8%) viewed CDIB cards in an ambivalent or neutral light. Participants stated that there were positive aspects as well as negative aspects to CDIB cards. They were positive for the same reasons others found them positive—they allowed access to services and programs reserved for Native peoples, and they kept those who were not Native from accessing these same services. However, the same negatives previously mentioned applied here as well; specifically, that CDIB cards do not really determine if someone is or is not Native, but rather it is that individual's connection to his or her culture and community. As stated by a twenty-six-year-old participant from California, "Somebody that's non-Native, if they're receiving that beneficial help from a tribe and they're not Native, then I think that's when the importance of the Certificate Degree of Indian Blood comes into play, because there's people out there who would sign up for that assistance and not even be Native. So, politically I think it's important . . . but among Native people, between each other, I don't think degree of Indian blood is important."[27]

The conflicting complexities surrounding blood quantum and CDIB cards were discussed by a thirty-nine-year-old participant from the Southern Plains. He stated,

I got mixed feelings on them because . . . you know . . . you're settling something down to genetics. I do think that because, at least in the last 20 years, because of the popularity of Indians, there needs to be something to set them apart or else every little hippie kid that thinks Indians are cool . . . next thing you know, they're an Indian. Because of that government-to-government relationship, those separate tribes are separate sovereign entities. . . . One of the core aspects of sovereignty is being able to choose who your people are that belong to that sovereign. And whereas the CDIB is essentially a federal government tool, rather than say, a membership card from a tribe, it is still used by those tribes to determine who's a member. You know, so, I think in respect, it's important. At the same time, I think when you are using it for the sole purpose for determining membership, you leave out a population of individuals who for some reason or another may not be eligible for that CDIB, as well as the fact that when you become a member of those tribes, they only count the blood quantum of that particular tribe. And what happens is you've got individuals that are essentially walking pan-Indians who have so many separate tribes within them . . . because of this paperwork . . . his blood's diluted. And so, there's good, there's bad.[28]

A participant from the Northeast explained:

Because of the geographic area I live in and because there are so many people claiming to be something they're really not and who really don't have any type of connection to a tribe. In that sense, you know, I think CDIBs are a good thing. On the flip side of the coin . . . I find it interesting that we're the only group of people who have to prove who we are. To the best of my knowledge, no one who is African-American has to have a card or something to show that's who they are. They just say that's who they are and people believe them.[29]

One participant, a forty-three-year-old from the Great Lakes, was fairly to the point when she said she, personally, had not had a CDIB card affect her one way or another. She said, "So, I have a card. . . . So far in my life it hasn't made much of a difference until recently. . . . Because I'm way off of the reservation, as far as where I live . . . there was never anything available to me. . . . I found a clinic down in Detroit that helps, and with me having my card, helped me get a little extra medical. Otherwise I haven't known too many differences yet that have affected me positive or negative."[30]

Conclusion

Pewewardy (2003) states:

> I see blood quantum as a double-edged sword, and people have no identity without that degree of blood. The more blood, the more power or validity that they think they have. I see blood quantum as a tool devised by dominant society to further divide and negate Indigenous Peoples. I see people who have married outside of the tribal communities, and their grandchildren have no tribal recognition because of blood quantum. Their own people strip their identities because they have bought into this system. (87)

Overall, Native peoples' opinions on blood quantum and CDIB cards are as varied as Native peoples themselves. *Native 24/7* participants saw both the good and bad aspects. Negative feelings seemed to connect to beliefs that blood quantum and CDIB cards were tools of the US federal government designed to continue colonial practices and ultimately get rid of Native peoples. Additionally, many participants also pointed to the fact that blood quantum and CDIB cards are not Native concepts and ideas, and that Indians are the only racial or ethnic group that needs a card to prove identity.

There were also many *Native 24/7* participants who viewed blood quantum and CDIB cards positively. These positive feelings were mainly linked to accessing tribal and federal governmental services and proof of Indian ancestry. A participant from the Eastern Band of Cherokee Indians explained, "I believe that's very important. It separates us from all the wannabees. It separates us from all the ones that say they're Indian and can't prove it. Our blood is what makes us Cherokee . . . our forefathers is what makes us who we are."[31]

However, the majority of participants viewed blood quantum and CDIB cards in dualistic and conflicting light; some things about blood quantum

and CDIB cards are good, while other things are not. As noted by a participant from the Southern Plains,

> I think they can be good or bad. Bad in a sense that it tends to . . . may be simi-
> lar to something that the Jews went through . . . sort of identifying people that
> may sort of set them up for a mass extinction, or that may set them up to put
> them through a sort of negative social transformation . . . an automatic label to
> sort of face scrutiny. But it's also good, in a sense, that it offers unique benefits
> that may be offered by institutions, such as the government, to your tribe. . . .
> It certainly has helped me in . . . getting scholarships . . . grants and such. And
> it is also important to know what you are, so you can identify yourself as one
> (Native). So, yeah, it can be good or bad.[32]

Notes

1. We are not using the terms race and ethnicity in the manners the US federal government typically does. Rather we are using the anthropological definitions
where race is defined as a false biological category based on phenotypes, such as skin
color, hair color, hair texture, eye color, eye shape, nose shape, and so forth. Ethnicity, on the other hand, is typically defined as a shared common identity, a distinct
language or dialect, and a distinct culture tied to land, resources, modes of produc-
tion, oral and written histories, worldview, as well as other characteristics, common
among members of a group within a broader society.

2. 25-year-old female from a California urban community.

3. 45-year-old female from a California urban community.

4. 63-year-old male from a Southern Plains rural community.

5. 28-year-old man from a Southeast reservation community.

6. 26-year-old male from a Southern Plains reservation community.

7. 53-year-old female from a Southwestern community.

8. 36-year-old female from a Southeast reservation community.

9. 70-year-old female from a Southern Plains urban community.

10. 19-year-old male from a Great Lakes reservation community.

11. 42-year-old female from a Great Lakes reservation community.

12. 30-year-old female from a Great Lakes reservation community.

13. 47-year-old female from a Great Lakes urban community.

14. 27-year-old female from a Southern Plains reservation community.

15. 53-year-old female from a Great Basin and Plateau urban community.

16. 55-year-old male from a Great Lakes urban community.

17. 30-year-old female from a Southwestern reservation community.

18. 26-year-old male from a Southwestern urban community.

19. 32-year-old male from a Southern Plains urban community.

20. 31-year-old female from a Southern Plains urban community.

21. 29-year-old female from a Southwestern reservation community.

22. 18-year-old female from a Great Basin and Plateau urban community.
23. 30-year-old male from a Southwestern reservation community.
24. 19-year-old female from a Great Basin and Plateau urban community.
25. 72-year-old female from a Northern Plains reservation community.
26. 48-year-old female from a Northern Plains reservation community.
27. 26-year-old male from a California urban community.
28. 39-year-old male from a Southern Plains urban community.
29. 39-year-old female from a Northeastern urban community.
30. 43-year-old female from a Great Lakes urban community.
31. 30-year-old male from a Southeastern reservation community.
32. 24-year-old male from a Southern Plains rural community.

CHAPTER SEVEN

~

"Football and Mascots"

What We Have Learned

Mikey Rousseau jumped up and down in his cleats and pounded his helmet to his head. This was it. He was ready. The scout from the University of Iowa, his dream school, was out there, waiting to see him. To see him beat the state record for passing yards in a season and win the state championship. To see HIM—a kid from the middle of nowhere on the rez. He knew, if he could only play this one last game right, he could get a scholarship, be the first in his family to go to college, be the kid who got out, got educated and came back and made a difference. Him—the kid who no one thought could do it, raised by Grandma with more aunts and uncles who were his age and younger than brothers and sisters of anyone he knew. The kid whose mom died during childbirth and whose dad was who knows where smoking meth with his buddies. This was the night he was going to prove everyone wrong, prove that he was better than everyone thought and he was READY. Coach said it was time to go. He ran to the front of the line and led his team out onto the field, shouting with his teammates, ready to take on those damn urban kids from the Mascot school—Center City High with their fighting Chiefs.

Mikey burst through the banner that said, "Show them who the real Chiefs are." He immediately saw the protesters with the signs and shirts proclaiming, "Not Your Mascot" and "You're Not Honoring Me." There was Grandma in her mascot shirt, at the head of the line, yelling louder than anyone else. He made eye contact with her and then ran harder onto the field. He could do it. He could do it for her.

While he warmed up with the team, he heard the argument breaking out. Parents from his own town, supposedly fans of his, were yelling at the mascot protesters, also supposedly fans of his. These other parents, those protesting the protesters, were talking about the real problems on reservations—suicide, alcohol, drugs, diabetes, domestic abuse, lack of running water and electricity in the rural homes (*like his sometimes*, Mikey thought). Those are the real issues, these new protesters proclaimed. And they were right. And the mascot people were right, too. It's really offensive to treat someone like they're the same as the animal mascots for other teams. And both sides could agree that everything was a problem. It was all about priorities. But did they have to talk about all of that at his game? Really—at this game? All he could think about was doing what he needed to do so that he could leave and come back to fix those problems.

Then the cops showed up. Rez cops, people from his own community, with views on both sides of the protesters. And they told everyone to calm down and watch the game. But instead of listening, one of the protesters, he couldn't tell from which side, threw a punch at a cop and all hell broke loose. Mikey couldn't tell who did what, but it was a brawl and it looked like everyone was involved. Then the arrests started and Grandma was with them. She wasn't going to get to see him play. He made eye contact with her one more time as she left the stadium in handcuffs and she mouthed the words, "I'm sorry. I'm proud of you." Then she was gone; something to deal with later.

Mikey refocused. He saw the other team down the field and scanned the players. They were from a city two hours away and they had everything. Public transportation to get them to school. Hospitals right down the street. Full grocery stores with everything they could want, even convenience stores if you didn't want to go the extra two blocks to the grocery store. Ambulances that stayed at their games to wait and see if anyone got hurt rather than taking calls all over the rez during the game because they were the only show in town. He could admit it. He was jealous. But he was going to win tonight, even with their star safety, that fake Indian Jake Curry, whose great-grandmother or someone was from his tribe. How could he even play for a team with that mascot and go to that school? I mean really, did anyone honestly think he was Native? With that dirty blond hair and blue eyes? Yeah, he went to powwows, even learned some grass dancing, but that's not being a real Indian. That's not what culture is. That's not being from the rez and living it every day. You wouldn't even know he was Native if he didn't tell every reporter he ran into. Probably trying to get a scholarship—cash in on that CDIB card he didn't deserve to own. *Doesn't matter*, he told himself, *tonight is my night and he can't take it away from me.*

Jake stood on the sideline watching the fight. What the hell was this about? Why did his own people hate him and his team? They didn't pick the damn mascot. He even wrote a piece for the school paper about why it was wrong. It didn't mean anything and no one cared, but he tried. And the fight didn't even include people from his school; everyone was from the rez. What was with these people? They're like crabs in a bucket. If they could just agree and deal with one problem at a time, maybe things would get done. Plus, these were people who got to learn their culture from day one. Be around it every day of their lives. Learn their language and religion from elders. Not get called a "pretend-ian" or "wanna-be NDN." Don't they know how good they have it? Focus, he told himself, they can't get to you. This game is too important. The scouts are out there, even the one from the University of Oklahoma. He could play there, he knew it. There, he could be someone and he could learn the history of his people. They even taught his language.

He had tried to learn it, but there weren't any speakers around him and his Mom wouldn't let him go hang out on the rez. She had left there after being called a half-breed too many times and seeing all the problems poverty caused. She had fallen in love with a white guy, married him, and left the rez. They didn't have a lot of money, but they were able to get jobs in the city and made a happy life for themselves, if not particularly lavish. If only she understood his need to learn about where he came from. Sure, she was ok with him going to powwows, but she didn't understand why he wanted to learn the culture so bad. She had been through so much and was still called a "prairie nigger" in their racist city so much that she told people she was part Mexican—that was better than Indian. She didn't see the good that could come of him spending any real time with Indians. It was all too painful for her. At least if he went to college and learned language and culture there, he could show her that it wasn't all about poverty, drugs, alcohol, and abuse. He would do it. He would be the first in his family to go to college. And he would make a difference for all the People who were pushed away from their communities just because they weren't 100% Indian. I mean, who really was 100% anymore? His family just admitted it unlike others.

Ok, it was time to go out for the coin toss. He stepped onto the field with his two other co-captains and met the Braves from the rez school (yeah, Braves, like that's not an Indian mascot). He saw their QB—Mikey Rousseau—among the four captains they sent out and felt the need to stop him from getting that state passing record. He could do it. He was averaging 12 interceptions per season and had 15 this year. Maybe not as good as high school national record holder Baron Jackson (62 total, 16 per year), but pretty damn good. He stared into Mikey's eyes for the entire coin toss, which they won, and elected to receive. And so it begins, he thought to himself . . .

End of the first quarter, score 14–13 Braves. Mikey could feel it; they were going to win and he was on his way to his state record, with already 75 passing yards. But that one interception from Jake Curry was going to haunt him.

Half-time, score 34–24 Chiefs. Jake ran into the locker room pumped up. He saw the scout from Oklahoma watching his two interceptions in two quarters, the second a run for a TD. If only the line could sack Rousseau; that kid was amazing.

End of the third quarter, score 41–41. This was getting crazy. Incredible game and Mikey looked amazing, but he had been intercepted twice in the first half, including one for a touchdown. He had to admit it, Jake Curry was good. If that hadn't happened, they'd be winning. At least he was still within range of that state record and he looked good. He knew Iowa would be fools not to take him. He was going to get out, get educated, and help his community.

Fourth quarter, 2 minutes to go, score 41–41. Man, that was a tough quarter. Jake hadn't had an interception during the second half at all, but he still looked good. He was going to talk to that recruiter and he was going to go to Oklahoma. He was going to major in Native American Studies, learn his culture, and learn his language. And then he was going to go back home and start an urban Indian center to help all the other kids like him.

Fourth quarter, 30 seconds to go, score 41–41. The ball is snapped and Mikey gets it and prepares to throw the Hail Mary so this doesn't go into overtime. His receiver is open and he launches the ball down the field. Jake sees the pass and sprints toward it. He leaps . . .

Catherine Thomas, unpublished 2021

Who wins? Does Mikey get his record? Does Jake intercept and send the game into overtime? Does either one go to the school of his dreams and help his people? And, who is more Indian? The answers to the first three questions really do not matter. Both played a great game and have a good shot at getting into school with a scholarship, maybe even the school of their dreams. And maybe, hopefully, they both go back to their communities and make a difference. Or maybe they wind up at the same school, ultimately becoming best friends and work together to help Native people. That would make a great Lifetime movie but does not typically reflect reality. What does reflect reality are the thoughts running through both Mikey's and Jake's heads. This is a work of fiction, but the scenes that play out are all too real. We are now back to the question with which we started *Native 24/7*: who is an Indian?

Comanche-Kiowa scholar Cornel Pewewardy (2003) has a take on this important and controversial concept:

It is difficult to define one's self culturally, tribally, spiritually, emotionally, mentally and so forth. Moreover, the trauma that has occurred over my lifetime is part of my healing journey. As an Indigenous person, I try to understand the present condition of Indigenous Peoples is a direct result of intergenerational deficits, benefits, grief and injury. I see that trauma and response to the pain of the emotional, spiritual, mental, physical, and tribal rape in many people. I see Indigenous People inflicting the same on their own and other tribal people. I see Indigenous People using their tribal identities and spirituality as a shield against others. They bring it out when it is necessary to protect them from facing themselves and taking responsibility for their own healing and definition. (86–87)

While Pewewardy is speaking primarily about himself, similar thoughts and perspectives emerged throughout the interviews and in the responses from *Native 24/7* participants. One young participant noted that being Native, "It's more than just a self-identity. It's who I am and it's what I relate to as a person, as a human being."[1] Another participant simple stated, "It's who I am. . . . I've known nothing else."[2]

Overall, while many of the quotes from *Native 24/7* participants were brief and often tautologies, the brevity and circular thinking did not diminish the power of these quotes, nor did they change the focus or importance that being Native is core to who participants are and how they experience the world. "It's the whole center post of my identity. It means everything. Without it I wouldn't be me."[3] "It's who I am. . . . It's who I grew up as. It's just me."[4]

The common theme here is that, in reality, the answer to our primary question is simple—an Indian is an individual, growing up in the midst of multiple cultures and worldviews, with many different influences and views on what it means to be a Native person in the United States in contemporary society. An Indian is a human being, and as such, each Indian is as unique as any other individual on the planet. After nearly a decade of work from concept inception to completion of the study, analysis and writing, we learned what we already knew, as is true in many research projects. Native people are a hugely heterogeneous group with widely varying beliefs, values, worldviews, and every demographic factor you can name. To reduce them to a single category is not fair to their diversity, but is the reality of conducting research, just like people from all over the continent of Asia who have moved to the United States are grouped together as Asian Americans. The difference is that they are not asked to prove who they are; we believe them.

None of our participants said that what defined them as a Native American was carrying a CDIB card, though for many individuals, CDIB cards were important. None of our participants said that the way they look defined them as an American Indian, though discussions did turn to the heterogeneity of what an Indian looks like. None of our participants said that participation in any one activity defined them as belonging to their tribe, though participation in multiple cultural activities was highly valued. None of them said speaking a Native language was the primary defining factor of Indigeneity, though it was considered important, when possible, to speak a Native language. Participants tied their identities to that amorphous category of "culture" that some academics no longer wish to consider a useful factor for analysis and to pieces of culture like spirituality, teachings from parents and elders, language, and participation in cultural activities.

What does this mean for researchers working with Native communities? It means that there is no question that can be asked that tells you if your participants are *really* Native. There is no scale that can adequately measure Indigeneity because there is no one way to be Indigenous. So, we came full circle, back to the tautology, "An Indian is a Native American person," or something like that. If researchers really want to ensure that the people they are enrolling in their studies are American Indians, the simplest answer is to ask them, the same way you ask someone if they are White or Black. And believe them.

Notes

1. 23-year-old female from a Great Lakes urban community.
2. 53-year-old female from a California urban community.
3. 68-year-old female from a Plateau reservation community.
4. 45-year-old female from a Southern Plains rural community.

Bibliography

Adese, Jennifer, Zoe Todd, and Shaun Stevenson. 2017. "Mediating Métis Identity: An Interview with Jennifer Adese and Zoe Todd." *Media Troupes eJournal* 7 (1): 1–25.

Aldred, Lisa. 2000. "Plastic Shamans and Astroturf Sun Dances: New Age Commercialization of Native American Spirituality." *American Indian Quarterly* 24 (3): 329–352. https://doi.org/10.1353/AIQ.2000.0001.

Alfred, Taiaiake, and Jeff Corntassel. 2005. "Being Indigenous: Resurgences against Contemporary Colonialism." *Government and Opposition* 40 (4): 597–614. https://doi.org/10.1111/j.1477-7053.2005.00166.x.

Amorth, Gabriele. 1999. *An Exorcist Tells His Story.* San Francisco: Ignatius Press.

Balu, Rebekah. 1995. "Indian Identity: Who's Drawing the Boundaries?" *Compleat Lawyer* 12 (4): 10–12.

Basso, Keith H. 1996. *Wisdom Sits in Places: Landscape and Language among the Western Apache.* Albuquerque: University of New Mexico Press.

Bee, Robert. 1999. Personal communication. University of Connecticut, Storrs, Connecticut.

Bernard, H. Russell. 2017. *Research Methods in Anthropology: Qualitative and Quantitative Approaches*, sixth edition. New York: AltaMira Press.

Bhabha, Homi K. 1985. "Signs Taken for Wonders: Questions of Ambivalence and Authority under a Tree outside Delhi, May 1817." *Critical Inquiry* 12 (1): 144–165. https://doi.org/10.1086/448325.

Brenner, Elise M. 1980. "To Pray or to Be Prey: That Is the Question Strategies for Cultural Autonomy of Massachusetts Praying Town Indians." *Ethnohistory* 27 (2): 135–152. https://doi.org/10.2307/481224.

Brubaker, Rogers, and Frederick Cooper. 2000. "Beyond 'Identity'." *Theory and Society*, 29(1): 1–47. https://doi.org/10.1023/A:1007068714468.

Bureau of Indian Affairs. 2017a. Bureau of Indian Affairs Certificate of Degree of Indian Blood or Alaska Native Blood Instructions. www.bia.gov/cs/groups/xraca/documents/text/idc1-029262.pdf.

Bureau of Indian Affairs. 2017b. Frequently Asked Questions. www.bia.gov/FAQs/index.htm.

Bureau of Indian Affairs. 2017c. Who We Are. www.bia.gov/WhoWeAre/index.htm.

Bureau of Indian Affairs. 2019. Genealogy. www.bia.gov/bia/ois/tgs/genealogy.

Bureau of Indian Affairs. 2021. US Department of the Interior: Indian Affairs. www.bia.gov.

Castells, Manuel. 2011, "A Network Theory of Power." *International Journal of Communication* 5: 773–787.

Chidester, David. 2014. *Empire of Religion*. Chicago: University of Chicago Press.

Colmant, Stephen A. 2000. "US and Canadian Boarding Schools: A Review, Past and Present." *Native Americas* 17 (42): 24.

Conklin, Beth A. 1997. "Body Paint, Feathers, and VCRs: Aesthetics and Authenticity in Amazonian Activism." *American Ethnologist* 24 (4): 711–737. https://doi.org/10.1525/ae.1997.24.4.711.

Cornille, Catherine. 2010. *Many Mansions?: Multiple Religious Belonging and Christian Identity*. Eugene: Wipf and Stock Publishers.

Cornsilk, David. (2008). African-Native American Forum, 08/02/2008, https://www.afrigeneas.com/forume/index.cgi/md/read/id/28936/sbj/cdib/.

Corntassel, Jeff. 2003. "Who Is Indigenous? 'Peoplehood' and Ethnonationalist Approaches to Rearticulating Indigenous Identity." *Nationalism and Ethnic Politics* 9 (1): 75–100. https://doi.org/10.1080/13537110412331301365.

Cross, Suzanne L., Angelique Day, and Lisa G. Byers. 2010. "American Indian Grand Families: A Qualitative Study Conducted with Grandmothers and Grandfathers Who Provide Sole Care for Their Grandchildren." *Journal of Cross-Cultural Gerontology* 25(4): 371–383. http://dx.doi.org/10.1007/s10823-010-9127-5.

Daley, Christine M., and Sean M. Daley. 2003. "Care of American Indians and Alaska Natives." In *Cross-Cultural Medicine*, edited by Judy Ann Bigby, 95–128. Philadelphia: American College of Physicians.

Daley, Christine M., K. Allen Greiner, Niaman Nazir, Sean M. Daley, Cheree Solomon, Stacy L. Braiuca, T. Edward Smith, and Won S. Choi. 2010. "All Nations Breath of Life: Using Community-Based Participatory Research to Address Health Disparities in Cigarette Smoking among American Indians." *Ethnicity and Disease* 20 (4): 334–338.

Daley, Christine M., Aimee S. James, Randall S. Barnoskie, Marcia Segraves, Ryan Schupbach, and Won S. Choi. 2006. "'Tobacco Has a Purpose, Not Just a Past': Feasibility of Developing a Culturally Appropriate Smoking Cessation Program for a Pan-Tribal Native Population." *Medical Anthropology Quarterly* 20 (4): 421–440. https://doi.org/10.1525/maq.2006.20.4.421.

Davis, F. James. 2010. *Who Is Black?: One Nation's Definition*. University Park: Penn State Press.

Davis, Jenny L. 2015. "Intersections of Religion and Language Revitalization." In *The Changing World Religion Map*, edited by Stanley D. Brunn, 1091–1101. New York: Springer.

De Castro, Eduardo Viveiros, Museu Nacional, and Rio de Janeiro. 2015. "Who Is Afraid of the Ontological Wolf?: Some Comments on an Ongoing Anthropological Debate." *The Cambridge Journal of Anthropology* 33 (1): 2–17. https://doi.org/10.3167/ca.2015.330102.

Deloria, Vine, Jr. 1969, 1988. *Custer Died for Your Sins: An Indian Manifesto*. Norman: University of Oklahoma Press.

Deloria, Vine, Jr. 1973. *God Is Red*. New York: Grosset & Dunlap.

Deloria, Vine, Jr. 1992. "Is Religion Possible? An Evaluation of Present Efforts to Revive Traditional Tribal Religions." *Wicazo Sa Review* 8 (1): 35–39. https://doi.org/10.2307/1409362.

Deloria, Vine, Jr. 2006. *The World We Used to Live In: Remembering the Powers of the Medicine Men*. Wheat Ridge: Fulcrum Publishing.

DeMallie, Raymond J. 1982. "The Lakota Ghost Dance: An Ethnohistorical Account." *Pacific Historical Review* 51 (4): 385–405. https://doi.org/10.2307/3639782.

DeMallie, Raymond J. 1984. *The Sixth Grandfather: Black Elk's Teachings Given to John G. Neihardt*. Lincoln: University of Nebraska Press.

Denetclaw, Pauley. 2017. "Data Shows Huge Reduction in Dine' Speakers." Navajo Times: *Dine' Bi Naaltoos*, November 16, 2017. navajotimes.com/reznews/data-shows-huge-reduction-in-dine-speakers.

Ehala, Martin. 2018. *Signs of Identity: The Anatomy of Belonging*. London and New York: Routledge.

Endangered Languages Project. 2021. Languages Map. endangeredlanguages.com/#/4/43.300/-2.104/0/100000/0/low/mid/high/unknown.

Enos, Tony. 2017. "8 Things You Should Know about Two Spirit People." *Indian Country Today*, March 28, 2017. indiancountrytoday.com/archive/8-misconceptions-things-know-two-spirit-people.

Erikson, Erik H. 1966. "The Concept of Identity in Race Relations: Notes and Queries." *Daedalus* 95 (1): 145–171.

Escobar, Arturo. 2008. *Territories of Difference: Place, Movements, Life, Redes*. Durham: Duke University Press.

Fixico, Donald. 1995. Introduction to the Reprint Edition. In *To Be an Indian: An Oral History*, edited by J. H. Cash and Herbert T. Hoover. St. Paul: Minnesota Historical Society Press.

Fletcher, Matthew L. M. 2012. "Tribal Membership and Indian Nationhood." *American Indian Law Review* 37 (1): 1–17.

Garroutte, Eva Marie. 2003. *Real Indians: Identity and the Survival of Native America*. Oakland: University of California Press.

Goeckner, Ryan T., Sean M. Daley, Jordyn Gunville, and Christine M. Daley. 2020. "Cheyenne River Sioux Traditions and Resistance to the Dakota Access Pipeline." *Religion and Society* 11: 75–91. http://dx.doi.org/10.3167/arrs.2020.110106.

Gooding, Susan Staiger. 1996. "At the Boundaries of Religious Identity: Native American Religions and American Legal Culture." *Numen* 43 (2): 157–183. https://doi.org/10.1163/1568527962598322.

Graeber, David. 2015. "Radical Alterity Is Just Another Way of Saying 'Reality': A Reply to Eduardo Viveiros de Castro." *HAU: Journal of Ethnographic Theory* 5 (2): 1–41. https://doi.org/10.14318/hau5.2.003.

Grande, Sandy. 2000. "American Indian Identity and Intellectualism: The Quest for a New Red Pedagogy." *International Journal of Qualitative Studies in Education* 13 (4): 343–359. https://doi.org/10.1080/095183900413296.

Grande, Sandy, Timothy San Pedro, and Sweeney Windchief. 2015. "Indigenous Peoples and Identity in the 21st Century: Remembering, Reclaiming, and Re-generating." In *Multicultural Perspectives on Race, Ethnicity, and Identity*, edited by Elizabeth Pathy Salett and Dianne R. Koslow, 105–122. Washington, DC: The National Association of Social Workers.

Gustafson, Hans. 2016. "Descandalizing Multiple Religious Identity with Help from Nicholas Black Elk and His Spirituality: An Exercise in Interreligious Learning." *Journal of Ecumenical Studies* 51 (1): 80–113. http://dx.doi.org/10.1353/ecu.2016.0000.

Hall, Laura, Tanya Shute, Parveen Nangia, Mikaela Parr, Phyllis Montgomery, and Sharolyn Mossey. 2020. "Indigenous Fathering and Wellbeing: Kinship and Decolonial Approaches to Health Research." *Diversity of Research in Health Journal* 3: 97–112. https://doi.org/10.28984/drhj.v3i0.303.

Hart, Michael A. 2010. "Indigenous Worldviews, Knowledge, and Research: The Development of an Indigenous Research Paradigm." *Journal of Indigenous Social Development* 1: 1A.

Irwin, Lee. 1997. "Freedom, Law, and Prophecy: A Brief History of Native American Religious Resistance." *American Indian Quarterly* 21 (1): 35–55. https://doi.org/10.2307/1185587.

Israel, Barbara A., Amy J. Schulz, Edith A. Parker, and Adam B. Becker. 1998. "Review of Community-Based Research: Assessing Partnership Approaches to Improve Public Health." *Annual Review of Public Health* 19: 173–202. https://doi.org/10.1146/annurev.publhealth.19.1.173.

Jacobs, Michelle R., and David M. Merolla. 2017. "Being Authentically American Indian: Symbolic Identity Construction and Social Structure among Urban New Indians." *Symbolic Interaction* 40 (1): 63–82. https://doi.org/10.1002/symb.266.

Jasper, James M. 1997. *The Art of Moral Protest: Culture, Biography, and Creativity in Social Movements*. Chicago: University of Chicago Press.

Johnson, Hayley. 2017. "#NoDAPL: Social Media, Empowerment, and Civic Participation at Standing Rock." *Library Trends* 66 (2): 155–175. http://dx.doi.org/10.1353/lib.2017.0033.

Kohn, Eduardo. 2015. "Anthropology of Ontologies." *Annual Review of Anthropology* 44: 311–327. https://doi.org/10.1146/annurev-anthro-102214-014127.

Kottak, Conrad P. 2016. *Mirror for Humanity: A Concise Introduction to Cultural Anthropology*, tenth edition. New York: McGraw-Hill Education.

Krol, Debra. 2018. "Should the BIA Get Out of the Blood Degree Business?" *Indian Country Today*, June 28, 2018. www.newsmaven.io/indiancountrytoday.

Lee, Tanya. 2018. "7 Most Popular Native American Languages in U.S." *Indian Country Today*, September 13, 2018. indiancountrytoday.com/archive/7-most-popular-native-american-languages-in-us.

Levy, Jerrold E., Raymond Neutra, and Dennis Parker. 1988. *Hand Trembling, Frenzy Witchcraft, and Moth Madness: A Study of Navajo Seizure Disorders*. Tucson: University of Arizona Press.

Liddell, Jessica L., Catherine E. McKinley, Hannah Knipp, and Jenn Miller Scarnato. 2021. "She's the Center of My Life, the One That Keeps My Heart Open: Roles and Expectations of Native American Women." *Affilia* 36 (3): 357–375. https://doi.org/10.1177%2F0886109920954409.

Light, Harriett K., and Ruth E. Martin. 1986. "American Indian Families." *Journal of American Indian Education* 26 (1): 1–5.

Looking Horse, Arvol. 2003. "Looking Horse Proclamation on the Protection of Ceremonies." Oneida, NY.

Magnat, Virginie. 2012. "Can Research Become Ceremony? Performance Ethnography and Indigenous Epistemologies." *Canadian Theatre Review* 151: 30–36. https://doi.org/10.3138/ctr.151.30.

Makosky Daley, C., Aimee S. James, Ezekiel Ulrey, Stephanie Joseph, Angel Talawyma, Won S. Choi, K. Allen Greiner, and M. Kathryn Coe. 2010. "Using Focus Groups in Community-Based Participatory Research." *Qualitative Health Research* 20 (5): 697–706. https://doi.org/10.11/1049732310361468.

Mann, Henrietta. 2004. "Of This Red Earth." In *A Will to Survive: Indigenous Essays on the Politics of Culture, Language, and Identity*, edited by Stephen Greymorning, 47–58. Boston: McGraw-Hill.

Martin, Joel W. 2001. *The Land Looks After Us: A History of Native American Religion*. Oxford: Oxford University Press.

Masuzawa, Tomoko. 2005. *The Invention of World Religions: Or, How European Universalism Was Preserved in the Language of Pluralism*. Chicago: University of Chicago Press.

McComb Sanchez, Andrea. 2020. "Resistance through Secrecy and Integration: Pueblo Indians, Catholicism, and the Subversion of Colonial Authority." *Religion* 50 (2): 196–214. https://doi.org/10.1080/0048721X.2020.1713514.

Mihesuah, Devon A. 1998. "American Indian Identities: Issues of Individual Choices and Development." *American Indian Culture and Research Journal* 22 (2): 193–226. https://doi.org/10.17953/aicr.22.2.9341w76528071x3j.

Mitchell, Don. 1995. "There's No Such Thing as Culture: Towards a Reconceptualization of the Idea of Culture in Geography." *Transactions of the Institute of British Geographers* 20 (1): 102–116. https://doi.org/10.2307/622727.

Murphy, James. 2017. "Beyond 'Religion' and 'Spirituality': Extending a 'Meaning Systems' Approach to Explore Lived Religion." *Archive for the Psychology of Religion*, 39 (1): 1–26. https://doi.org/10.1163%2F15736121-12341335.

Mutchler, Jan E., Lindsey A. Baker, and SeungAh Lee. 2007. "Grandparents Responsible for Grandchildren in Native-American Families." *Social Science Quarterly* 88 (4): 990–1009. http://dx.doi.org/10.1111/j.1540-6237.2007.00514.x.

Neihardt, John G. 1996. *Black Elk Speaks*. Woodstock: Dramatic Publishing.

Orsi, Robert A. 2006. *Between Heaven and Earth: The Religious Worlds People Make and the Scholars Who Study Them*. Princeton: Princeton University Press.

Orsi, Robert A. 2010. *The Madonna of 115th Street: Faith and Community in Italian Harlem, 1880–1950*. New Haven: Yale University Press.

Paper, Jordan D. 1988. "The Sacred Pipe: The Historical Context of Contemporary Pan-Indian Religion." *Journal of the American Academy of Religion* 56 (4): 643–665. https://doi-org.eres.qnl.qa/10.1093/jaarel/LVI.4.643.

Parezo, Nancy. 1996. "The Dine' (Navajos): Sheep Is Life." In *Paths of Life: American Indians of the Southwest and Northern Mexico*, edited by Thomas Sheridan and Nancy Parezo, 3–34. Tucson: The University of Arizona Press.

Parks Canada: Government of Canada. 2018. Pukaskwa National Park: An Anishinaabe Creation Story. www.pc.gc.ca/en/pn-np/on/pukaskwa/culture/autochtone-indigenous/recit-story.

Pearce, Lisa D., and Arland Thornton. 2007. "Religious Identity and Family Ideologies in the Transition to Adulthood." *Journal of Marriage and Family* 69 (5): 1227–1243. http://dx.doi.org/10.1111/j.1741-3737.2007.00443.x.

Peek, Lori. 2005. "Becoming Muslim: The Development of a Religious Identity." *Sociology of Religion* 66 (3): 215–242. https://doi.org/10.2307/4153097.

Peterson, L. 2013. "'Kill the Indian, Save the Man,' Americanization through Education: Richard Henry Pratt's Legacy." Colby College, Honors Theses, Paper 696. https://digitalcommons.colby.edu/honorstheses/696/.

Pewewardy, Cornel. 2003. "To Be or Not to Be Indigenous: Identity, Race, and Representation in Education." *Indigenous Nations Studies Journal* 4 (2): 69–91.

Phan, Peter C. 2003. "Multiple Religious Belonging: Opportunities and Challenges for Theology and Church." *Theological Studies* 64 (3): 495–519. https://doi.org/10.1177/004056390306400302.

Pink, Sarah. 2005. "Dirty Laundry. Everyday Practice, Sensory Engagement, and the Constitution of Identity." *Social Anthropology* 13 (3): 275–290. https://doi.org/10.1111/j.1469-8676.2005.tb00391.x.

Pink, Sarah. 2011. "From Embodiment to Emplacement: Re-thinking Competing Bodies, Senses and Spatialities." *Sport, Education and Society* 16 (3): 343–355. https://doi.org/10.1080/13573322.2011.565965.

Polletta, Francesca, and James M. Jasper. 2001. "Collective Identity and Social Movements." *Annual Review of Sociology* 27 (1): 283–305. https://doi.org/10.1146 /annurev.soc.27.1.283.

Postsecondary National Policy Institute (PNPI). 2020. Native American Students in Higher Education. pnpi.org/native-american-students/.

Public Religion Research Institute. 2021. The American Religious Landscape in 2020. www.prri.org/research/2020-cences-of-american-relgion/.

Rice, Emma S., Emma Haynes, Paul Royce, and Sandra C. Thompson. 2016. "Social Media and Digital Technology Use among Indigenous Young People in Australia: A Literature Review." *International Journal for Equity in Health* 15 (1): 81. https:// doi.org/10.1186/s12939-016-0366-0.

Robbins, Rockey, Avraham Scherman, Heide Holeman, and Jason Wilson. 2005. "Roles of American Indian Grandparents in Times of Cultural Crisis." *Journal of Cultural Diversity* 12 (2): 62–68. http://dx.doi.org/10.26536/PJVQ7990.

Roberts, Michelle Voss. 2010. "Religious Belonging and the Multiple." *Journal of Feminist Studies in Religion* 26 (1): 43–62. https://doi.org/10.2979/fsr.2010.26.1.43.

Schmidt, Ryan W. 2011. "American Indian Identity and Blood Quantum in the 21st Century: A Critical Review." *Journal of Anthropology*, 1–9. https://doi .org/10.1155/2011/549521.

Smith, Jonathan Z. 1998. "Religion, Religions, Religious." *Critical Terms for Religious Studies*, 269–284.

Smith, Linda T. (2013). *Decolonizing Methodologies: Research and Indigenous Peoples.* London: Zed Books Ltd.

Soto-Márquez, José G. 2019. "'I'm Not Spanish, I'm from Spain': Spaniards' Bifurcated Ethnicity and the Boundaries of Whiteness and Hispanic Panethnic Identity." *Sociology of Race and Ethnicity* 5 (1): 85–99. https://doi.org/10.1177 %2F2332649218766388.

Spruhan, Paul. 2006. "A Legal History of Blood Quantum in Federal Indian Law to 1935." *South Dakota Law Review* 51: 1–50.

Spruhan, Paul. 2018. "CDIB: The Role of the Certificate of Degree of Indian Blood in Defining Native American Legal Identity." *American Indian Law Journal* 6 (2), Article 4.

Steinmetz, Paul B. 1998. *The Sacred Pipe: An Archetypal Theology.* Syracuse: Syracuse University Press.

Stewart, Omer C. 1987. *Peyote Religion: A History.* Norman: University of Oklahoma Press.

Stoeber, Michael. 2020. "Indigenous and Roman Catholic Canonizations of Nicholas Black Elk: Postcolonial Issues and Implications of Black Elk Speaks." *Theological Studies* 81 (3): 605–630. https://doi.org/10.1177%2F0040563920953835.

Stolzman, William. 1991. *The Pipe and Christ: A Christian-Sioux Dialogue,* fourth edition. Chamberlain: Tipi Press.

Tam, Benita Y., Leanne C. Findlay, and Dafna E. Kohen. 2017. "Indigenous Families: Who Do You Call Family?" *Journal of Family Studies* 23 (3): 243–259. https://doi /10.1080/13229400.2015.1093536.

Taylor, Robert J., and Linda M. Chatters. 2010. "Importance of Religion and Spirituality in the Lives of African Americans, Caribbean Blacks and Non-Hispanic Whites." *The Journal of Negro Education* 79 (3): 280–294.

Thornton, Russell. 1996. "Tribal Membership Requirements and the Demography of 'Old' and 'New' Native Americans." In *Changing Numbers, Changing Needs: American Indian Demography and Public Health*, edited by Barney Cohen, Ronald R. Rindfuss, and Gary D. Sandefur, Chapter 5. Washington, DC: National Academies Press.

Thornton, Russell. 2005. "Native American Demographic and Tribal Survival into the Twenty-first Century." *American Studies* 46 (3/4): 23–38.

Tuck, Eve, and K. Wayne Yang. 2012. "Decolonization Is Not a Metaphor." *Decolonization: Indigeneity, Education, and Society* 1 (1): 1–40.

United States Census Bureau. 2020. Subject Definitions. United States Department of Commerce. www.census.gov/programs-surveys/cps/technical-documentation /subject-definitions.html#family.

United States Census Bureau. 2021. Race and Ethnicity in the United States: 2010 Census and 2020 Census. census.gov/library/visualizations/interactive/race-and -ethnicity-in-the-united-state-2010-and-2020-census.html.

Van Bragt, Jan. 2010. "Multiple Religious Belonging of the Japanese People" In *Many Mansions? Multiple Religious Belonging and Christian Identity*, edited by Catherine Cornille, 7–19. Eugene: Wipf and Stock Publishers.

Van Niekerk, Brimadevi. (2018). "Religion and Spirituality: What Are the Fundamental Differences?" *HTS: Theological Studies* 74 (3): 1–11. https://doi.org /10.4102/hts.v74i3.4933.

Virtanen, Pirjo Kristiina. 2015. "Indigenous Social Media Practices in Southwestern Amazonia." *AlterNative: An International Journal of Indigenous Peoples* 11 (4): 350–362. https://doi.org/10.1177%2F117718011501100403.

Weaver, H. N. 2001. "Indigenous Identity: What Is It, and Who Really Has It?" *American Indian Quarterly*, 25 (2), 240–255. https://doi.org/10.1353/aiq.2001.0030.

White Bison. 2002. *The Red Road to Wellbriety*. Colorado Springs: White Bison.

White Hat, Albert, Sr., and John Cunningham. 2012. *Life's Journey—Zuya: Oral Teachings from Rosebud*. Salt Lake City: University of Utah Press.

Wilson, Shawn. 2008. *Research Is Ceremony: Indigenous Research Methods*. Black Point: Fernwood Publishing.

Wilson-Hokowhitu, Nālani. 2019. *The Past before Us: Moʻokūʻauhau as Methodology*. Honolulu: University of Hawaii Press.

Windchief, Sweeney, and Timothy San Pedro. 2019. *Applying Indigenous Research Methods: Storying with Peoples and Communities*. London and New York: Routledge.

Wissler, Clark. 1927. "The Culture-Area Concept in Social Anthropology." *American Journal of Sociology* 32 (6): 881–891.

Wolfe, P. 2006. "Settler Colonialism and the Elimination of the Native." *Journal of Genocide Research* 8 (4): 387–409. https://doi.org/10.1080/14623520601056240.

Yellow Bird, Michael. 1999. "Indian, American Indians, and Native Americans: Counterfeit Identities." *Winds of Change: A Magazine for American Indian Education and Opportunity* (Winter): 86.

Zinnbauer, Brian J., Kenneth I. Pargament, Brenda Cole, Mark S. Rye, Eric M. Butter, Timothy G. Belavich, Kathleen M. Hipp, Allie B. Scott, and Jill L. Kadar. 1997. "Religion and Spirituality: Unfuzzying the Fuzzy." *Journal for the Scientific Study of Religion* 36 (4): 549–564. https://doi/10.2307/1387689.

Index

Page numbers with an *f* refer to a figure or a caption; *t* refers to a table; and *n* refers to an endnote.

preferences, *33t*, 35; and views on CDIB cards, *102t*, 104–5

US-Dakota War of 1862, 70n14

US government: assimilation goals, 95; tribal relationships with, 94–95

US history books, Native history omission, 48

Wakonda (God), 67

Weaver, Hilary, 26, 37

Wheeler-Howard Act (Public Law 73-383), 96–97

White Mountain Apache blood quantum requirements, 96

Wissler, Clark, 4

Wounded Knee descendant, 47

Yang, K. Wayne, 109–10

Yellow Bird, Michael, 28, 29

~

About the Authors

Sean M. Daley is cofounder and director of the Institute for Indigenous Studies at Lehigh University. He is also an associate professor in community and population health in Lehigh University's College of Health. He is an applied sociocultural anthropologist and ethnographer with expertise in American Indian Studies, community-based participatory research, and cultural tailoring. Much of his work lies at the intersections of religion, spirituality, and health. He has been working with Native peoples since 1995 and has worked with Native communities in Arizona, Connecticut, Kansas, Montana, New Mexico, and South Dakota, as well several other states. His work has focused heavily on contemporary American Indian health, wellness, and spirituality. He has also worked in the areas of Native law and policy, identity, education, and the environment. He is also the cofounder and the codirector of the American Indian Health Research and Education Alliance, a 501(c)(3) not-for-profit organization dedicated to improving health and educational attainment in American Indian communities through quality participatory research and education.

Christine Makosky Daley is professor and chair of the Department of Community and Population Health in the College of Health at Lehigh University, as well as the cofounder of the Institute for Indigenous Studies. She is an applied medical anthropologist, mixed methodologist, and community-based participatory researcher by training and has been working with American Indian communities since her undergraduate career. Her primary area of research interest is reducing American Indian health disparities. She conducts community-based participatory research in which community members are involved in all phases of the research, from concept inception through design, analysis, and dissemination. Her research includes tobacco prevention and control, cancer screening, weight loss, behavioral epidemiology, environmental health, health literacy, community education, and, most recently, mental health and the ethical conduct of research. She is also the cofounder and the codirector of the American Indian Health Research and Education Alliance.

~

About the Contributors

Ryan Goeckner is a senior research scientist in the Institute for Indigenous Studies. His research interests fall at the intersection of Native resilience, futurities, and identity, as well as Indigenous recreational tobacco cessation, mental health and addiction, college preparation for reservation youth, and contemporary American Indian identities. Ryan is also a doctoral candidate in cultural anthropology at The Ohio State University. His dissertation project seeks to understand how practices of resilience throughout the COVID-19 pandemic in American Indian communities evidence the futures imagined by these communities.

Jason Hale (Prairie Band Potawatomi) is a senior research scientist in the Institute for Indigenous Studies. His current research includes reducing smoking among American Indians through the development and implementation of culturally tailored smoking cessation interventions. He is also actively working on research projects with American Indian tribal communities to understand the knowledge, attitudes, beliefs, and behaviors of American Indians surrounding COVID-19. Hale's other research interests and community engagement work include weight loss, nutrition, and American Indians in higher education.

~

About the Research Team

Charley Lewis (Paiute/Navajo) is a senior research scientist in the Institute for Indigenous Studies. His research focuses on Native health disparities and working with American Indian communities; environmental health, tobacco cessation, mental health and suicide, cancer education, as well as the development of culturally tailored health interventions. He is also a doctoral candidate in the Department of Population Health at the University of Kansas Medical Center. His dissertation research is concentrated on COVID and predictors of vaccination among Native peoples and vaccine policy implementation on reservations.

Joseph Pacheco (Quechua/Cherokee) is an assistant professor in the Department of Community and Population Health and a faculty member of the Institute for Indigenous Studies at Lehigh University. He has had extensive experience working in the field of public health and has conducted prevention and implementation research for over ten years. His research focuses on commercial and traditional tobacco use and tobacco control policy views among American Indians. He also works with Indigenous populations in the realm of environmental health to improve access to care, reduce barriers to care, and develop new and innovative interventions to reduce health disparities.